W9-BXZ-457

Praise for
Baseball as a Road to God

John Sexton, the president of New York University, has served in that position since 2001. Before being named NYU's president, he served as dean of the NYU School of Law for fourteen years. President Sexton is past chairman of the American Council on Education, the New York Academy of Sciences, and the Commission on Independent Colleges and Universities of New York. He is a fellow of the American Academy of Arts and Sciences, a member of the Council on Foreign Relations, and has served as the chairman of the board of the Federal Reserve Bank of New York. He received a PhD in History of American Religion from Fordham University, a JD magna cum laude from Harvard Law School, and has ten honorary doctorates, including one from the oldest Catholic university in the world, Katholieke Universiteit Leuven. In addition to his executive duties at NYU, he teaches four full courses each academic year, making him one of the only university presidents to teach a full faculty schedule.

Thomas Oliphant was a columnist for *The Boston Globe* for more than forty years and is a *New York Times* bestselling author. He has been part of the Baseball as a Road to God seminar for years. He lives in Washington, DC.

Peter J. Schwartz is a *Bloomberg News* contributing writer, former reporter at *Forbes* and legal fellow at NYU. He was the first student ever enrolled in the Baseball as a Road to God seminar. He lives in New York City.

BASEBALL

as a Road TO GOD

SEEING BEYOND THE GAME

JOHN SEXTON

with Thomas Oliphant and Peter J. Schwartz

AVERY
an imprint of Penguin Random House
New York

an imprint of Penguin Random House LLC
375 Hudson Street
New York, New York 10014

Previously published in hardcover by Gotham Books
First trade paperback edition, March 2014
Copyright © 2013 by John Sexton

Most Avery books are available at special quantity discounts for bulk purchase for sales promotions, premiums, fund-raising, and educational needs. Special books or book excerpts also can be created to fit specific needs. For details, write SpecialMarkets@penguinrandomhouse.com.

The Library of Congress has catalogued the hardcover edition as follows:

Sexton, John.
Baseball as a road to God : seeing beyond the game / John Sexton with Thomas Oliphant and Peter J. Schwartz.
p.   cm.
Includes index.
ISBN 978-1-592-40754-5
1. Baseball—Religious aspects—Christianity.   I. Oliphant, Thomas.
II. Schwartz, Peter J.   III. Title.
GV867.S58   2013   2012029685
796.35701—dc23

ISBN 978-1-592-40864-1 (paperback)

Printed in the United States of America
      5   7   9   10   8   6

Book design by Spring Hoteling

For Lisa, who showed us the way
and
for Jed and Katie, who walk it

John SEXTON - impressive bio!

P.3 - Thomas Nagel, NYU philosopher, Mind and Cosmos

5 - Book based on JS course of same name -

6 - Charlie WINANS, HS mentor

7 - the "ineffable"

8 - Mircea Eliade - the Sacred & Profane

9 - the Mysterium

- Karen Armstrong, The Case for GOD

HIEROPHANY

9 - "prayer changes people, NOT Things"

123 - Thomas Jefferson

CONTENTS

This book takes the reader on a remarkable spiritual journey, using the secular sport of baseball to explore subjects ordinarily associated with religion: prayers, altars, sacred space, faith, doubt, conversion, miracles, blessings, curses, saints, and sinners. There is magic in these pages. I have loved baseball all my life, but never before did I fully comprehend the sacred dimensions of that love.

The book opens on October 4, 1955, a day long etched into the memory of baseball fans. John Sexton and his friend Bobby Douglas are on their knees, offering prayers before the radio in the hope that the Brooklyn Dodgers, after years of agonizing losses, might finally beat the New York Yankees and win their first World Series.

I, too, had raced home from school that day so that I could hear the end of the game in the familiar surroundings of my home, with my mother by my side. And I, too, prayed for victory. "Please, God, let this year be the year!" Our collective prayers were answered when the game ended and

Vin Scully delivered the message Brooklyn fans had waited generations to hear: "Ladies and gentlemen, the Brooklyn Dodgers are the champions of the world." My mother and I were momentarily speechless. As Sexton observes, some feelings are ineffable, too overwhelming to be expressed in words. I jumped up and threw my arms around my mother, tears streaming down our cheeks.

Storytelling is at the heart of this book—stories that reveal the connections between the joys of loving baseball and the joys of a spiritual life. Seasonal ceremonies of rebirth and renewal figure largely in both realms, as do rituals, traditions, and superstitions. Sexton tells the story of a prolonged slump endured by Dodger first baseman Gil Hodges. In the midst of the slump, a priest in Brooklyn abandoned his scheduled sermon, asking his congregation instead to pray for Gil Hodges. When Hodges began to hit, the parishioners believed they were responsible. I knew better. I had given Gil Hodges the Saint Christopher's medal blessed by the pope that I had won in a catechism contest by knowing the seven deadly sins. Since Saint Christopher was the patron saint of travel, I was certain that my medal had guided Hodges safely around the bases.

The Dodgers' move to Los Angeles in 1958 stands at the center of *Baseball as a Road to God*. This betrayal of staggering dimensions leads Sexton to an absorbing discussion of spiritual conversion. "Conversion is not for the faint of heart," he argues. "It is a difficult process, requiring effort and perseverance." Some Brooklyn fans rejected baseball entirely. Others consigned themselves to follow their old team from a distant shore. The arrival of the New York Mets in 1962 eased the way for many, allowing a peaceful transfer of allegiance without losing the sense of community engendered by a hometown team.

John Sexton experienced a more dramatic conversion. For nearly two decades, still living in New York, he continued to root for his beloved Dodgers. After his son, Jed, fell in love with the New York Yankees, however, the "unthinkable" happened. The bond between father and son trumped Sexton's old loyalty to the Dodgers. He experienced a "moment of conversion," finding a new faith in the team he had once hated—he became and still remains a tried-and-true Yankee fan.

My own conversion followed a different path. After the Dodgers abandoned me, I could not follow baseball for eight years, until I moved to Boston and went to Fenway Park. There it was again, a "sacred place," to use Sexton's words, so reminiscent of Ebbets Field: a fervent crowd contained in a stadium scaled to human dimensions, the players so close it seemed almost as if you could touch them. Nor could I have found a new team more reminiscent of the old Brooklyn Dodgers: perpetual bridesmaids year after year. Nonetheless, I became an irrational Red Sox fan and have passed that love to my three sons. We have had season tickets for more than thirty years, but even though my conversion is complete, there are days when I sit with my sons and imagine myself a young girl once more in the presence of my father, watching the players of my youth on the grassy field below: Jackie Robinson, Pee Wee Reese, Roy Campanella, Duke Snider. As Sexton rightly argues, the "intertwining of past and present" is at the heart of baseball's appeal.

Through this book, I came to a better understanding of the miraculous Red Sox championship in 2004. Sexton was seated near a group of Yankee VIPs in the fourth game of the championship series. With the Sox down three games to zero and behind 4–3 in the bottom of the ninth, several of the Yankee brass began to leave, an act Sexton perceived as one of the deadly sins—the haughty pride that often "precedes a fall." The Sox went on to win that game and the three that followed, before crushing St. Louis in the World Series.

While reason suggests that Boston won the World Series because it had better pitching than St. Louis, I found in Sexton's discussion of faith and doubt a far more interesting explanation. Faith and doubt, he argues, are at the core of both religion and baseball. For years, Red Sox fans had been consumed with doubt and darkness. For years, the players had shared "the institutional memory" of losing seasons. After the miraculous comeback against the Yankees, however, the team played like boys—high-spirited, fun-loving, confident boys, enjoying every minute of the game. They believed so strongly in themselves that they cast a spell upon us, and once we truly believed in them, our belief redoubled their strength. Whatever happened, we had faith they would see us through. And they surely did, creating what Sexton calls "mystical moments" that will remain in our memories forever.

THE KNOTHOLE GANG[*]

In the basement of my family's home, my friend Bobby "Dougie" Douglas and I knelt and prayed with all the intensity we could muster, grasping between us in dynamic tension each end of a twelve-inch crucifix we had removed from the wall.

We prayed before a radio instead of an altar, which broadcast the sounds of Game Seven of the 1955 World Series instead of hymns. We had sprinted to my home the instant the nuns released us from our eighth-grade class— sprinted as fast as we could, driven by our knowledge that, with three innings to go, the Brooklyn Dodgers were leading the New York Yankees by the perilous score of 2–0. All we and every other living Dodgers fan had known to that

---

[*] *The Knothole Gang* was the mother of all pregame shows, preceding Brooklyn Dodger broadcasts in the fifties. Hosted by Happy Felton, a very large, bespectacled vaudeville performer, it featured Little Leaguers who sought tips from featured Dodgers and then threw and fielded in fabled Ebbets Field to win prizes and tickets to upcoming games. To appear on it was the highest point of many a New York childhood.

point were the pain and anguish of bitter disappointment. Three innings and that finally could change.

In that basement, seconds felt like hours as we prayed and lived through each agonizing pitch; through the pinch-hitting appearance of an injured Mickey Mantle with one man on and two out in the bottom of the seventh inning (he popped out); through the tension an inning later as the Yankees put two men on with two out (the young Dodger pitcher Johnny Podres struck out Hank Bauer on a high fastball to end the threat). Release did not come until Yankee rookie Elston Howard tapped the final pitch (a changeup) weakly to short—indeed, not until shortstop Pee Wee Reese's low throw had been snared by the outstretched glove of Gil Hodges at first base.

For three innings, time had slowed; but in that moment it froze: The Brooklyn Dodgers had won the World Series! Seven decades of waiting were over! Dougie raised his arms in exultation, releasing the crucifix, whereupon the laws of physics drove the head of Christ into my mouth, chipping my front tooth. I wore that chipped front tooth, unrepaired, as a visible memento for nearly fifty years.

All these years later, every pitch of those last three innings is etched in memory—not because our prayers were answered (at least not in any way that I would acknowledge today). That day lives for me still because it was magical (better yet, mystical): the improbable triumph, yes; but even more important, the intensity of the hope and ecstasy that Dougie and I shared.

For the two of us, baseball and our still-forming Catholic faith were not connected literally; nonetheless, though we did not appreciate it at the time, baseball that day displayed some of the profound and complex elements that constitute religion. We were transported to a plane familiar to "the faithful"—to a place where faith, hope, and love were as much on display as Podres's arm.

October 4, 1955. For me and millions of others, a sacred day. Why? Hard to put into words. Impossible to capture completely in our limited vocabulary.

But we do have a word for something that defies reduction to words: *ineffable*. We cannot define the ineffable, even though we can experience and "know" it profoundly (I *know* Lisa, my wife, loves me). And we can evoke it—in story or "myth" (not *myth* as "falsehood," but *myth* in the original, sublime sense of the word).

We live in the age of science; the wonders of knowledge and the results created by it surround us. Its possibilities give us hope for a better world. In some quarters, however, the promise of science has spawned what might be called "scientism"—a belief that just because something is said (*ipse dixit*, as scholars like to say), science captures or will capture all that there is to know in any sense of that word. I do not believe this.

As Rabbi Abraham Joshua Heschel wrote: "God is not a scientific problem, and scientific methods are not capable of solving it. . . . [T]he problem of God is not only related to phenomena within nature but to nature itself; not only to concepts within thinking but to thinking itself. It is a problem that refers to what surpasses nature, to what lies beyond all things and all concepts. The moment we utter the name of God we leave the level of scientific thinking and enter the realm of the ineffable."

My New York University colleague Thomas Nagel, who is widely recognized as one of the most thoughtful philosophical minds of our time, argues forcefully in his most recent book, *Mind and Cosmos,* that our present methods of gaining knowledge likely will be supplemented by new tools. As he put it:

It is perfectly possible that the truth is beyond our reach, in virtue of our intrinsic cognitive limitations, and not merely beyond our grasp in humanity's present stage of intellectual development. But I believe that we cannot know this, and that it makes sense to go on seeking a systematic understanding of how we and other living things fit into the world. In this process, the ability to generate and reject false hypotheses plays an essential role. I have argued patiently against the prevailing form of naturalism, a reductive materialism that purports to capture life and mind through its neo-Darwinian extension. . . . I find this view antecedently unbelievable—a heroic triumph of ideological theory over common sense. The empirical evidence can be interpreted to accommodate different comprehensive theories, but in this case the cost in conceptual and probabilistic contortions is prohibitive. I would be willing to bet that the present right-thinking consensus will come to seem laughable in a generation or two—though of course it may be replaced by a new consensus that is just as invalid. The human will to believe is inexhaustible.

I agree. The story of the advance of knowledge has been and will be a continuing translation of the unknown to the known; and it surely is correct that science as we know it today is but one of the tools our successors will have to continue the process.

Beyond what is unknown today, there is something that is plainly unknowable, ineffable, no matter how hard we try to figure it out. This dimension of human experience touches some of the most important features of our existence.

Stephen Jay Gould, scientist and baseball fan, once referred to science and religion as "nonoverlapping magisteria." I think he had it just right; and unlike the priests or disciples of scientism, I comfortably embrace *both* the wonders of the first magisterium (science) and the ineffable wonders of the second (the religious or spiritual).

Today, as for thousands of years, it is possible to find meaning beyond words everywhere—and in this domain beyond words, the religious or spiritual resides. In an age of gigabytes and picoseconds, we tend to live too quickly and to miss much that we might see. Baseball, as it turns out, can help us develop the capacity to see through to another, sacred space. Indeed, the more we come to appreciate the sport's intricacies and evocative power, the clearer it is that it shares much with what we traditionally have called religion.

Exploring the elements of a religious and spiritual life is a thread running through courses that I have taught over nearly five decades. I was put on this earth to be in a classroom; I am one of the few university presidents who teaches a full faculty schedule. This book grew out of one of my courses, one called Baseball as a Road to God. Like any good creation story, it begins in a garden.

It was November 21, 1999, and I was standing in the garden of Villa La Pietra, NYU's fifty-seven-acre campus in Florence, Italy. I was then dean of the School of Law, and we had just finished three days hosting seven heads of government, led by the President of the United States.

We had received the wheels-up signal, meaning all the leaders were aloft in their jets and no longer our responsibility, and we had begun a party for those who had worked on the event. Just then, an impious student (one of the volunteer workers) approached me: "I understand you're a big baseball fan," he said. "I think the sport is silly and I don't understand why anybody would waste time on it."

"You are among the great unwashed," I replied, invoking a favorite line of the mystical Charlie Winans, my mentor during high school and long afterward.

Charlie is central to this story, literally and spiritually. Father William O'Malley, one of his colleagues at the remarkable Jesuit high school I attended, caught the essence of Charlie when he wrote: "Charlie had the body of Orson Welles, the voice of James Earl Jones, and the soul of Francis of Assisi. Charlie could drink till three but be up for mass at six. He was the first fully *real*-ized Christian I ever met."

In and out of class, Charlie urged us, a group of Brooklyn Catholic working-class boys, to "play another octave on the piano" (taste the food you have not tasted, sing the song you have not sung, visit the place you have never visited). He pressed us to find wonder in places and things that seemed unremarkable on the surface but that could be transformed by careful inspection and introspection.

Channeling Charlie and relishing the student's challenge, I made him a proposal: "If you will read twelve books that I choose next semester, I will direct you in an independent study at the end of which you will realize that baseball is a road to God." He did, and I did, and it didn't take long before word of our work together spread. Other students asked to take "the course," and it became a seminar that I have taught for ten years.

My work with my students and the course that has evolved from it has never been about proselytizing them for religion or for God (whatever that word means to you). At first, it was about forcing them to develop their understanding of what the words *religion* and *God* could mean, so that they could make considered decisions about whether they wished to pursue either; baseball was the vehicle for developing that understanding, as we would probe each week whether, for the characters we encountered in the readings, it operated as a religion or caused them to encounter God (in any sense of the word). I was and remain indifferent to whether a student came to view baseball as a road to God (the indefinite article clearly signals it is not *the* road for everyone). Over the years, however, I became very interested in helping the students to develop their capacity for contemplation, sensitivity, awareness, and mystical intensity. Baseball, it turns out, is a wonderful laboratory.

Not long ago, the PBS journalist Bill Moyers featured the seminar as part of an interview he did with me. He taped during two classes, in one asking a student to explain the content of the course. "You know," the student replied, "my friends ask me to explain it all the time. Is it about baseball? Not exactly. Is it about God? Not exactly. So what is it about? If you want to know, you'll have to come and experience it for yourself. It's ineffable."

There's that word again: ineffable. That which cannot be defined or captured by words, though poetry and music and art sometimes come close. As Rabbi Heschel put it: "By the ineffable we do not mean the unknown as such; things unknown today may be known a thousand years from now. By the ineffable we mean that aspect of reality, which by its very nature lies beyond our comprehension and is acknowledged by the mind to be beyond the scope of the mind." Like what Dougie and I experienced that day in 1955 when the ball landed in Hodges's glove.

If there is the rational, the irrational, and the nonrational (or the known, the unknown, and the unknowable), the ineffable lives in the last category. And it is our purpose to explore it. We use tools employed by scholars of religion to analyze the game of baseball and how its fans experience it. What we find is that there are similarities—surprising similarities. Baseball evokes in the life of *its* faithful features we associate with the spiritual life: faith and doubt, conversion, blessings and curses, miracles, and so on. For some, baseball really is a road to God.

The superficial similarities between baseball and religion are many and varied: a ballpark is a church and a ball game is a mass; there are three strikes to an out and three outs to an inning, another set of holy trinities; or there are nine positions on the field, nine innings in a game, and nine muses in Greek mythology. There are also more poetic connections between baseball and religion, ones evoked by the beauty of the outfield grass or the serenity of a high-arching fly ball. Still others verge on silliness. For example, the mistaken claim made by the character Annie in the movie *Bull Durham* that there are one hundred and eight beads on a Catholic rosary and one hundred and eight stitches in an official baseball (actually, the number of beads varies depending on the rosary, and the number of stitches in a baseball is two hundred and sixteen). The more revealing connections between baseball and the religious experience go much deeper than that.

Some of the most interesting writing on the nature of religion done in the last century is by Mircea Eliade, a professor at the University of Chicago (though not, safe to say, a fan of the nearby White Sox). Eliade chronicled the continuous human search for meaning and for vehicles capable of connecting believers to the sacred—what for them is experienced as holy. With thousands of examples drawn across time and place, he shows that the experience of the sacred is subjective. Each person in his own time, place, and context makes a choice, separating what is sacred *for him* from what is profane *for him*. Eliade's definition of the *sacred* and the *profane* is deliberately circular: The sacred is that which is not profane; the profane is that which is not sacred.

The sacred manifests itself, he tells us, in space and time; certain places, things, and actions evoke for a religious man the spiritual plane. And connecting to this ineffable domain forms the basis of the religious experience. Eliade called this phenomenon a hierophany (the shining through of the sacred). Such experiences are not the exclusive province of organized religion; as it turns out, we humans have developed a variety of ways (from yoga to a well-turned 6-4-3 double play) to transcend the mundane experience of every-day life.

And sometimes, we are transformed and/or transported in an utterly profound way. As Eliade wrote, the mundane and profane can become holy and sacred:

> It is impossible to overemphasize the paradox represented by every hierophany, even the most elementary. By manifesting the sacred, any object becomes *something else*, yet it continues to remain *itself*, for it continues to participate in its surrounding cosmic milieu. A *sacred* stone remains a *stone*; apparently (or more precisely, from the profane point of view), nothing distinguishes it from all other stones. But for those to whom a stone reveals itself as sacred, its immediate reality is transmuted into a supernatural reality. In other words, for those who have a religious experience, all nature is capable of revealing itself as cosmic sacrality. The cosmos in its entirety can become a hierophany.

He went on to say that the revealed sacred "effects a break in plane" and "makes possible ontological passage from one mode of being to another." That's a lot to come from a stone (or a baseball), but Eliade showed that, for us humans, it always has been such.

Rudolf Otto, whose work influenced Eliade, described the sacred as *mysterium tremendum et fascinans* (Latin for a "mystery, both fearful and fascinating"), that which is "wholly other" from what is experienced in ordinary life. This *mysterium* is an unknowable reality, incapable of being reduced to cognitive categories.

William James put it this way: "How infinitely passionate a thing like religion at its highest flights can be. Like love, like wrath, like hope, ambition, jealousy, like every other instinctive eagerness and impulse, it adds to life an enchantment which is not rationally or logically deducible from anything else." He adds that the essence of the religious experience, those highest flights, is found deeply within ourselves: "in feeling; and the recesses of feeling, the darker, blinder strata of character, are the only places in the world in which we catch real fact in the making and directly perceive how events happen."

The ineffable is experienced, not defined, revealing itself in moments of intense feeling. The setting is beside the point, be it a house of worship or a mountaintop or a ballpark. One label for the sacred (for *mysterium tremendum et fascinans*) is *God*. Used this way (the way I use it), the "God" involved is not the anthropomorphic deity who resides in green pastures.

Karen Armstrong, in her wonderful book *The Case for God*, put it well:

> The catechism definition I learned at the age of eight—"God is the Supreme Spirit, who alone exists of himself and is infinite in all perfections"—was not only dry, abstract, and rather boring; it was also incorrect. Not only did it imply that God was a fact that it was possible to "define" but . . . I was not taught to take the next step and see that God is *not* a spirit; that "He" has *no* gender; and that we have *no* idea what we mean when we say that *a* being "exists" who is "infinite in all perfections." The process that should have led to a stunned appreciation of an "otherness" beyond the competence of language ended prematurely.

The great theologian Paul Tillich, whom Armstrong also cites, captured the way we use the word *God* in my course:

The name of this infinite and inexhaustible depth and ground of all being is *God*. That depth is what *God* means. And if that word has not much meaning for you, translate it, and speak of the depths of your life, of the source of your being, of your ultimate concern, of what you take seriously without any reservation. Perhaps, in order to do so, you must forget everything traditional that you have learned about God, perhaps even the word itself. For if you know that God means depth, you know much about him.

In this book, we ask whether baseball, like Catholicism or Islam or peyote in the desert, can be a road to God—not *the* road to God for all, but *a* road to God for some. The traditional religions also have deep appeal to adherents but little or no appeal to others.

The essence of the agony and ecstasy Dougie and I experienced during the final innings on October 4, 1955, is not in the confluence of baseball and religion on a surface level—listening to a broadcast while clutching a crucifix—but is in its *depth*, the feelings and sensitivities that were evoked by the experience. During Podres's long walks to the mound, it was impossible not to wonder if he had a few more pitches in his tired left arm, to worry if too much was being asked of the twenty-three-year-old pitcher. After he threw his final pitch, after that last ground ball, we were released from all those years of misses and, as tension turned to joy, we celebrated with exultation worthy of the dervishes. In only three innings of baseball, all that: wonder, awe, hope, passion, heroism, and community.

And there are as many other examples as there are baseball storytellers. My journey along this road, from childhood to the cusp of old age, provides a less exhaustive list of hierophanies than Eliade marshaled in his comprehensive surveys of the world's religions; still, the entries are legion. For one more, let me jump forward nearly fifty years from that October day I knelt with Dougie praying for the Dodgers.

Strictly as baseball, it was one for the ages—the Yankees ahead three games to none in the 2004 American League Championship Series and ahead in the fourth game, 4–3, in the bottom of the ninth inning. As the Red Sox came to bat, Boston's Fenway Park was a funeral home. Seated behind the visitors' dugout in an enclave carved out for Yankee staff and a small group of fortunate fans, I could sense the brooding presence of the famous Curse of the Bambino. Three more outs and the Red Sox could count eighty-six years without a championship.

Suddenly, there was movement nearby. Several of the VIP Yankee fans around me were starting to leave, trying to beat the large crowd out of the ancient ballpark. Granted, an early exit seemed reasonable: The spirit of the Sox had been broken (the score the night before had been 19–8), the Yankees were ahead again, and the Red Sox were facing Mariano Rivera, the magnificent relief pitcher who had already retired the heart of their batting order an inning earlier while barely breaking a sweat. Still, it was troubling to see these VIPs so sure of their team's victory that they couldn't be bothered to stay and see it happen. It reeked of hubris, the sin of pride. Pride, one of the seven deadly sins. Pride, in the words of Proverbs, the "haughty spirit" that precedes a fall. More than one pair of eyes glared at them, including two pairs belonging to the polar opposites of Yankee celebrity, former New York mayor Rudolph Giuliani and filmmaker Spike Lee. I warned a friend and minority Yankee owner who got up to join those leaving: "If you go, you will reverse the Curse."

The bottom of the ninth began with a walk to Red Sox infielder Kevin Millar. I knew, along with everyone in the ballpark, that the pinch runner sent in to replace Millar at first base—speedy veteran Dave Roberts—would try to steal second. It was so obvious, we later learned, that Red Sox manager Terry Francona didn't even bother to give Roberts the steal sign; he simply winked at him as he left the dugout to enter the game.

Yankees manager Joe Torre also knew a steal attempt was coming, and he should have ordered a pitchout. But he didn't, and Roberts made it safely to second, where he was in a position to score the tying run on the single that followed. And that set the stage for Red Sox slugger David Ortiz's home run that won the game in the bottom of the twelfth inning.

Virtually the same thing happened the next night in Game Five to tie the score in the bottom of the eighth inning. The Red Sox won (this time with an Ortiz single) in the fourteenth inning, ending what was then the longest postseason game ever played, nearly six hours.

What followed, with the series back in New York, was just as dramatic: a pitching feat of epic courage by Red Sox veteran ace Curt Schilling in Game Six—his right ankle bleeding from last-minute surgical repairs—helped tie the series. And then the roof caved in on the suddenly hapless Yankees in a 10–3 seventh-game blowout. Schilling's red sock was later sent upstate to Cooperstown for display at the Hall of Fame, a relic if ever there was one. One week later, the Red Sox were world champions.

No serious case can be made that the departure of a few high rollers precipitated the unprecedented resurgence of the Sox. Still, the chain of events—including the sense of foreboding their departure induced in some of us—built moment by moment (think Ravel's *Boléro*) to an excruciatingly intense experience, ineffable at its core—a palpable feeing that there were higher forces at work. The consensus among experts and fans alike is that Mariano Rivera is the greatest reliever of all time. The statisticians will remind you that no reliever is so great that he never blows a lead and thus conclude that the Game Four collapse was simply a manifestation of the law of averages. But passionate fans, those who packed the ballpark that night and felt what was in the air, know differently.

While the teams and players on the field may change each autumn, the game's evocative power is continuous. Opening Day in the spring and the World Series in the fall are the bookends of baseball's liturgical time, and within the rituals of each season, fans are converted to believers; players, managers, and even owners become saints (or sinners); and events become part of a mythology, forever remembered and repeated with the solemnity of the most beloved sacred stories. And inevitably, each season brings its moments of heightened awareness—divergent from ordinary time and place—in which some discover a connection to something deeper than the ordinary. Such moments are remembered not merely for what they literally were but for what they evoked in those who experienced them.

Vantage point is critical. In baseball, as in religion, it is often very difficult to see through another person's eyes. Ecstasy for some is agony for others. In the autumn of 1951 when the New York Giants' Bobby Thomson hit his historic three-run home run to cap one of the most unlikely comebacks ever and abruptly end the Dodgers' season, my heart sank while those of friends all around me soared to inexpressible heights. But to be a baseball fan—even in youth— is to know that fortune can change in an instant. The next game or series or season could be the one.

Context was also central to the atmosphere that day in October 1955 when Dougie and I prayed for the Dodgers. Often, memories of past disasters and the feelings of accursedness that accompany them enhance the joy of the release from anguish that ultimate triumph provides. And sometimes, at least in retrospect, hope builds slowly to success in a way that makes success more beautiful.

The millions of Americans who endured the Brooklyn Dodgers until they ran away to Los Angeles in 1958 knew all about crushing failure. Incredibly, during the nine seasons ending in 1953, leaving out the war years, the Dodgers faced the Yankees in the World Series five times and lost each time, twice in seventh games; they lost the National League pennant three times on the very last day of the season. And the way they lost pivotal World Series games went beyond bizarre to seem fated: In one case, a catcher dropped a third strike; in another, a pitcher actually lost a ground ball in the sun; and in a third, a potential winning hit was caught at literally the last instant before it hit the ground.

Then came 1955 and Game Seven. Early on, while that crucifix was still hanging undisturbed on the wall in my bedroom, "signs" appeared, just as they did as the VIPs left Fenway in the bottom of the ninth inning forty-nine years later; to the careful observer on that fateful October 1955 day, events suggested the possibility of a different outcome.

In the bottom half of the third inning, the Yankees had runners on first and second with two out, with Gil McDougald batting and Yogi Berra up next. Swinging at a low pitch from Johnny Podres, McDougald sent a slow-bouncing ball to the right of third base. The Dodger third baseman, a young Don Hoak, froze, and the Yankee base runner, Phil Rizzuto, had simply to dodge the bouncing ball to get safely from second to third base, loading them all up for Berra. Unbelievably, however, he slid right into the ball, an automatic out, taking the Yankees out of the inning. The Dodgers started scoring the very next inning, and Podres pitched a shutout to give Brooklyn its first and only World Series title.

This was the kind of play that usually ruined the Dodgers; this kind of play never went their way; but that afternoon it did. The historical record is devoid of any indication that Dodgers fans read Mircea Eliade or Rudolf Otto, but to this previously unlucky mass, Rizzuto's slide was a hierophany—*mysterium tremendum et fascinans.*

Fans occasionally do experience these moments as divergent from the ordinary, as connected to another dimension. Not all fans. Not even most fans. Not all the time. But for some fans, these special moments touch the part of us where the mystics live.

It is through a collection of such experiences that my students and I have come to appreciate the jarring proposition that baseball can show us more about our world and ourselves than we might have thought. Or at the very least, it can demonstrate the benefits of living a little slower, of noticing a little more, and of embracing life's ineffable beauties—as that impious student in Florence eventually understood.

Once upon a time, a great author, poet, and fan sat in the bleachers of the original Yankee Stadium and saw more than a building and a baseball game.

From his outfield perch, John Updike studied the stately facades, the towering columns, and the expanse of gorgeous green grass in front of him.

"Distance brings proportion," he wrote in a poem first published in *The New Yorker* in 1956 during baseball's golden age. "From here the populated tiers as much as players seem part of the show."

Of course, Updike also saw a baseball game. But even as he watched the box score entries come to life before him with an eye that noticed "[Mickey] Mantle's thick baked neck," he connected to the received history of the game in the older men around him who once had watched "Hans" (his more famous nickname was Honus) Wagner play shortstop with his notoriously large "lobster" hands.

Most of all, he saw unity in time and place, in the nature

of the "show" (not coincidentally, the word many baseball people use for the major leagues). Old and young, past and present, change and constant, building and playing field, all viewed under a Bronx sky inspired Updike to see the unity in life. To him, it was an ideal way to spend an afternoon.

Baseball moves beyond ordinary space and time, as the poem tells us, in its flow of feelings and images. Updike invoked Taoism (the poem is titled "Tao in the Yankee Stadium Bleachers"), referencing Taoist parable, the great Tao teacher Chuang-tzu, and above all the "pureness" of the experience—" 'pure' in the sense of undisturbed water."

And he looked to the classics of the West as well. Baseball, in its totality, is "a constructed stage beast, three folds of Dante's rose"—suggesting the Italian poet's visions of heaven, hell, and purgatory.

The poem ends serenely: "The Inner Journey seems unjudgeably long when small boys purchase cups of ice and, distant as a paradise, experts, passionate and deft, wait while Berra flies to left."

It is a tough, demanding poem (one reason I assign it in my class). But its elements are accessible, if not familiar, to any fan who has embraced the whole show—whether in Yankee Stadium or the "friendly confines" of Chicago's Wrigley Field or Pittsburgh's long-gone Forbes Field or any other of baseball's venues.

Whether as stage, setting, or metaphor, we visit the ballparks for more than a game. For even a modestly passionate fan, much less a spiritual one, there is the tableau. It tugs at us, calling upon us to notice the details, to raise our awareness, to see deeply, and by so doing, to move beyond the obvious.

It is a composite, joining the ballpark and the game. In Eric Rolfe Greenberg's novel *The Celebrant*, there is a wonderful description of what happens on a line drive to left (by a player named Kopf) with a runner (Duncan) on second base:

> Here was all the intricate movement of a play in baseball: Duncan taking tentative steps toward third, then exploding into a full gallop as he saw that the ball would drop in front of Jackson; the left fielder dashing to the line of the hit, overrunning it slightly to ensure the freedom of his gloved left hand as he scooped the ball from the grass; shortstop Risberg aligning himself and raising his glove to offer Jackson a near target for his direct throw home; the third baseman to his station, the second baseman to his, and the catcher, Schalk, stripping the mask from his head and flinging it far away as Duncan turned third and headed home. And the forgotten portion of the plan: Kopf, the batter, rounding first and making for the extra base that a play at the plate would allow him.

So it is that a character in W. P. Kinsella's *The Iowa Baseball Confederacy* urges his son Gideon and the reader to watch closely the choreography of such plays:

> "Gideon, there's a lot more to watching a baseball game than keeping your eye on the ball. . . . [T]he real movement doesn't start until the ball is in play. *After* the ball is hit, *after* it has cleared the infield, especially if it is going for extra bases, you've got to train yourself to look back at the infield. While the outfielder is running down the ball, watch who is covering which base, watch to see who is backing up third and home. You'll be amazed at the amount of movement. Ah, Gideon, when everyone is in

motion it's like watching those delicate, long-legged insects skim over calm water. . . .

"You've got to watch the pitcher, Gideon. . . . and you'll appreciate why baseball is a combination of chess and ballet. Watch him back up the bases, watch him get across to first on a grounder to the right side, see how the first baseman leads him, tossing to an empty sack, trusting him to be there.

"When it looks like nothing is going on, choose a player and watch him react to every pitch, rising like water, receding like water. Watch a different player every inning. It takes a lot of years watching baseball to learn *not* to follow the ball every second. The true beauty of the game is the ebb and flow of the fielders, the kaleidoscopic arrangements and rearrangements of the players in response to a foul ball, an extra-base hit, or an attempted stolen base."

For Updike and legions of others who open themselves to such wonders, the sights and sounds of a day at the ballpark can summon an inner self, conjured as one moves through the park's entrance (the Great Hall at Yankee Stadium), crossing a threshold separating the "profane" world outside from the "sacred" world that lies inside its gates.

Updike viewed the old stadium from the center field bleachers. But its enormity was overwhelming from any vantage point. For my part, I remember how as a boy I felt awe as I walked the outfield after a game. In those more innocent days, at the Stadium and at a few of the other then-sixteen major league ballparks (the New York Giants' Polo Grounds, within sight directly across the Harlem River, was another), fans could walk the outfield grass (always watched carefully by the groundskeepers) after the game as they began their journey home. In those magical moments, we could examine up close the chalk-etched geometry of the field. Believe me, to pause on the grass in Yankee Stadium's short right field and stare at the area around first base, where Lou Gehrig once ruled, quickens the heart. And a few dozen steps farther into right field, where it was possible to touch the turf Babe Ruth once patrolled, it beats still faster. From the field, the facade and the columns were even more imposing. As hundreds of fans gazed in wonder, ushers had to urge them along. NYU's commencement is held annually at Yankee Stadium; and I must confess that, as I retrace those steps of long ago in the academic procession each year, I feel as much a baseball fan as a university president.

For some of us, a visit to the ballpark is a move from one state of being—the more familiar one—to another. It is a transformation, evoking a connection to something deep and meaningful. This is more than the simple, surface ob-servation that a stadium can be a church and the bleachers can be its pews; the stadium acts as what Eliade would call *axis mundi*—a channeling of the intersection between our world and the transcendent world, a place "sacred above all" that connects the ordinary and the spiritual dimen-sions. It is not that this evocative experience occurs for ev-eryone in every ballpark every time; but it can happen to anyone, in any ballpark, anytime. In this place, magic can happen, and the fan can be transported to a space and time beyond, to an experience we know profoundly but cannot put into words.

Stadiums sometimes are less majestic than Yankee Sta-dium, but several are famously intimate, linked to their com-munities by their own histories and traditions, representing much more than concrete and steel.

Only the spiritually numb would miss the wonder of Wrigley Field, one of only two stadiums (the other being Fenway Park) still standing from the construction binge that began early in the last century. Designed tastefully to fit into its residential neighborhood on the Second City's North Side (the stadium was built not for the Cubs but for the Chicago Whales of the Federal League, who played there for two years before folding), Wrigley is famous for its ivy-covered outfield walls; but there is much more to this great park.

The best way to approach Wrigley is by the stands in the left field corner. As you enter, you see the green ivy that defines the place, stretching around the outfield. This distinctive feature was the vision of a thirteen-year-old fan named Bill Veeck, whose father, a Chicago sports reporter, literally wrote his way to the presidency of William Wrigley's Cubs. When the boy eventually joined the team's management, he got to execute his vision, at one point even helping to plant the ivy. Today, a ball hit into the tangled greenery that is lost like an errant golf shot (it happens frequently) is an automatic double.

A bit to the right you see the giant scoreboard—also Bill Veeck's idea—still operated by hand and devoid of the instant replays that mark today's ballparks—and still untouched by a batted ball.

A little farther right you can see atop a building across the street the bleachers of the Lakeview Baseball Club, where fans watch the game from seats outside the park (you pay a stiff price for these Lakeview Club seats, though you still can watch the game for free from a number of the other buildings that ring the outfield). These unusual seats are marked by two huge signs, each featuring Latin. The first reads EA-MUS CATULI!, meaning "Go Cubs," and the second reads AC (as in *anno catuli,* the year of the Cubs) followed by a string of numbers representing the number of years since a division championship, since the last World Series appearance, and since the last world championship. In 2012, the AC sign was taken down for repairs, igniting a debate about whether the numbers should be restored or eliminated as too negative.

Tucked inside the grandstand is the oldest organ still in use in the major leagues, whose predecessor was actually the first one to produce one of baseball's distinctive sounds. There remains very little canned music at Wrigley Field today.

If you grab a hot dog and a beer (the favored brand is still Old Style), you can get it where the major leagues' first built-in concession stand stood.

And during the seventh-inning stretch when some favored guest, often a celebrity, leads the fans in "Take Me Out to the Ball Game," it continues a tradition started by the team's delightfully daffy broadcaster, the late Harry Caray (né Harry Christopher Carabina). Usually with a few Old Styles in him, he would lean precariously out of his booth, instantly recognizable in his thick black-rimmed glasses, wave an arm, and shout out: "And a one, and a two, and a three . . ." It still happens.

Walk toward home plate and you can, if you ask politely, sit for a minute or two in the legendary front-row seat that symbolizes the Cubs' long championship-missing drought—aisle 4, row 8, seat 113. That was where a lifelong Cubs fan, Steve Bartman, was sitting for Game Six of the National League Championship Series against the Florida Marlins on October 14, 2003—ninety-five years to the day from when the Cubs beat Detroit in 1908 to win their second consecutive World Series (they haven't won one since). With one out in the top of the eighth inning, five outs from the World Series, and the Cubs leading 3–0, the Marlins' Luis Castillo hit a high fly ball that twisted toward that seat, looking like easy pickings for left fielder Moises Alou. Oblivious to the oncoming Alou, and with headphones in place, Bartman reached for it, his hands just above Alou's outstretched glove. The ball glanced off Bartman's hand and fell to the ground. Alou was furious at the lost chance for an out, and the fluke play set off an eight-run Marlins inning. The next day, the Cubs lost Game Seven as well, and the Marlins went on to beat the Yankees in the World Series. It could have happened to anybody.

Walk a little farther and stop behind home plate, the actual site of as famous a home run swing as there is in the game's history. Babe Ruth stood on that spot during Game Three of the 1932 World Series. With two strikes against him, and with some very rough language from the Cubs' dugout ringing in his ears, the Babe gestured toward center field. What he meant remains a subject for debate (arguments are part of what makes baseball appealing), but Ruth hit the next pitch from the Cubs' Charlie Root into the very bleachers he had marked.

Wrigley is hallowed, sacred space. So, too, the onetime home of the Pittsburgh Pirates, the team that joined the Giants and the Cubs to dominate the National League during the first three decades of the twentieth century. Not far from downtown (in the Oakland section of the city), in a quiet courtyard on the campus of the University of Pittsburgh, a visitor in the right frame of mind can travel metaphorically to the America of his father or grandfather. Here is the site, lovingly memorialized, of Forbes Field, where the Pirates played from 1909 through 1970. They won two of their three seven-game World Series victories of this period here, among the most thrilling ever staged.

In the courtyard, there is a large section of the old brick wall from the cavernous ballpark's center field, complete with a flagpole right where the original stood. When Forbes Field opened, it was just barely the second stadium (Philadelphia's old Shibe Park was first by a nose) built with concrete and Pennsylvania's most famous product, steel. These new parks were such wonders of entertainment for ordinary working folks, they in fact often were called cathedrals.

The first year the park was open, the Pirates, led by Honus Wagner, nosed out Ty Cobb's Detroit Tigers in a tight series that still stirs arguments. And sixteen years later, against Walter Johnson's Washington Senators, they were the first team to win a World Series after trailing three games to one (it wouldn't happen again for more than thirty years).

Forbes Field is a wonderful example of baseball's historic role in American life. When the park opened, there wasn't much a steel-mill worker could afford to do in his precious free time, but he could afford to see a game; and folks dressed in suits and nice frocks to do so. When they got to the ballpark, they saw players who were just like them, not yet distanced by lucrative contracts and mass media attention. And they could root and celebrate and grieve—but, above all, enjoy and bond—with the team and one another.

The team meant a great deal to working families, especially recent immigrants. The Pirates' owner, Barney Dreyfuss, was himself an immigrant who had come from Germany and whose family made money in the liquor business. It was he who moved several of his best players there from the team he owned in Louisville; he helped negotiate the peace between the older National League and the upstart American League that created the modern majors; and he suggested celebrating the union with what became the World Series in 1903. (Pittsburgh lost that first Series, narrowly, to Boston.) It was also Dreyfuss who ripped down the Pirates' wooden grandstand downtown ballpark, Exposition Park, and built a new stadium at the end of a trolley line. It was a park built for working families, especially recent arrivals.

Pittsburgh was a natural place for immigrants to go, because they were certain to find work—extremely hard work and extremely low-paying. The typical immigrant in the early 1900s would make about fifteen dollars for a sixty-hour workweek. But hard as it was, every once in a while they would find their way to the ballpark and buy a seat for about twenty-five cents. Sometimes, if they saved their money, they could take their family.

And on the field they saw people like them—such as the revered Honus Wagner, one of nine kids whose father came from Germany to toil in the mills. Wagner himself dropped out of school at the age of twelve to go to work. Then came baseball. And how he played the game! With eight batting titles, more than seven hundred stolen bases, and a career batting average of .327, he was among the first five men inducted into the fledgling Hall of Fame in upstate New York (along with Ty Cobb, Babe Ruth, Walter Johnson, and Christy Mathewson, against whom he once got five hits in five at-bats). Only Cobb received more votes, and only a few more at that.

Naturally, there is a big statue of Wagner in Pittsburgh today. It originally stood outside Forbes Field; then in 1971, it was moved to Three Rivers Stadium; and finally, it was placed where it now stands outside the main entrance of PNC Park. Nearby there is another memorial, a section of the original Forbes Field outfield wall, from left-center field, complete with its old distance sign of 406 feet. The most important home run ever hit at Forbes Field, one that has to be on the short list of the most important in baseball history, sailed directly over that wall on October 13, 1960. When it did, for the first time ever, a World Series—and a seventh game no less—ended with a home run.

That historic blast was hit by the Pirates' second baseman, Bill Mazeroski—who was building a Hall of Fame career but who, truth be told, was not known at the time as a power hitter—to end possibly the most thrilling World Series game ever played. It was anything but a pitchers' duel. After multiple lead changes, comebacks, and bizarre plays, the score was tied 9–9 in the bottom of the ninth inning— as, of course, was the series (three games each) between the Pirates and the heavily favored New York Yankees.

Mazeroski, the first man up, faced the Yankee relief pitcher (normally a starter) Ralph Terry; he took the first pitch for a ball. When the second pitch came in over the middle of home plate, a bit more than waist high, Mazeroski jumped on it. The celebration of that swing, which brought glory after a thirty-five-year drought, continues to this day. People gather at the Forbes memorial every October 13 to play a tape of the radio broadcast. And a few years ago, a kinescope recording of the NBC television broadcast, thought to be lost forever, was discovered in pristine condition in the San Francisco wine cellar of a onetime minority owner who had the film made because—too nervous to watch in person—he went on vacation to Paris during the World Series. That owner was Bing Crosby.

A footnote to the story is that in the split second before Mazeroski's home run soared over the left-center field wall, it passed over the head of Yogi Berra. By then, the aging Yankee catcher had started to play left field. Berra, a noted poet of the oxymoronically obvious, once said that "it is tough to make predictions, especially about the future," an insight also attributed to nuclear physicist Niels Bohr. In any event, true to his aphorism, Berra would say after the game that he no more expected Mazeroski's blast than anyone else.

When Pirates fans congregate at the remaining piece of the Forbes Field wall, they see the monument as more than slabs of brick, and they arouse the deeper perception that religious man has brought to sacred spaces through the ages. The piece of wall may appear to be just that; but in reality it can be so much more.

Mircea Eliade's extensive studies of religion over millennia reveal that we always have elevated particular places to special (in some cases, sacred) status. Any place can create this sharp divergence from the ordinary to the sacred. This is hierophany: a touching of the transcendent plane. "Where the sacred manifests itself in space, *the real unveils itself,"* Eliade wrote. And that sacred space, deeply personal to each individual, may seem quite ordinary to others.

Present a stranger with pictures of a Lutheran church, Catholic basilica, mosque, and baseball field, and then ask which does not belong with the others. Just about everybody would single out the stadium. Eliade's point is that while this is the right answer for most, for others it is not. A universe of possibilities can stir a sense of the sacred; and yes, the special places of baseball can be such a catalyst. If we understand his point, we learn something about the nature of religion.

Baseball also has its sacred times. Times experienced by parent and child, brother and brother, friend and friend— whether sitting at a ballpark, following a broadcast (for many, ball games provide the soundtrack to summer), or deciphering a box score the day after a game.

By its very nature and rules, baseball operates outside of ordinary time; in fact, timelessness is at its essence. The length of an inning or game is not set by a clock; it shares the boundless framework of Eliade's sacred time: It is not linear, with a simple past, present, and future; it is cyclical, building and building again toward certain, quintessential moments.

For the religious, this cyclical liturgical time is marked by ritual and ceremony. The experience thus evoked is elevating, transporting the believer back to the original moment that is his spiritual root—*in illo tempore* (literally "in that time" that is revered). The customs and practices of almost every religious tradition reveal such moments—from the Advent and Lent of Christianity to the Jewish High Holy Days to Ramadan in Islam. As Eliade wrote, "Just as a church constitutes a break in plane in the profane space of a modern city, the service celebrated inside it marks a break in profane temporal duration."

For many fans, the most sacred times are Opening Day and the World Series. As the Hall of Fame infielder Rogers

Hornsby said, "People ask me what I do in winter when there's no baseball. I'll tell you what I do. I stare out the window and wait for spring."

Each spring, just before Easter and Passover, baseball elicits a sense of renewal. The cry "Wait'll next year" is prologue, replaced by hope. As Joe DiMaggio once said, "You always get a special kick on Opening Day, no matter how many you go through. You look forward to it like a birthday party when you're a kid. You think something wonderful is going to happen." The anticipation that has built during the off-season ends as the players finally take the field: The wait is over; the slate is clean. No matter last season's record, all now are tied at zero wins and zero losses, and even last year's most moribund squad can dream of being champion (and as the 1991 Atlanta Braves and Minnesota Twins attest, that dream can become reality).

For the first game of the season, ballparks often are dressed in red, white, and blue bunting. Sometimes the President of the United States appears, venturing to the pitcher's mound to toss a ceremonial first pitch, bringing baseball back to life. The long, dark nights of winter are over.

In Cincinnati, Opening Day is especially important. That city fielded the first all-professional team in 1869, and to honor that generative move, baseball's rulers have scheduled the Reds' first game at home each season for 124 years, two forgettable exceptions notwithstanding. Dormant for months, the streets surrounding the Great American Ball Park come alive, bustling with vendors hawking hot dogs, peanuts, and Cracker Jack. Father and son, mother and daughter walk hand in hand through a sea of red.

Inside, before the game begins, players and coaches assemble on each foul line and, according to baseball custom, are introduced one by one in order of the numbers stitched to the back of their uniforms (this does not happen again during the regular season). Heroes of the past are honored, and if five months earlier the home team won a championship, that pennant is raised to mark the achievement. A color guard marches onto the field carrying another pennant, the star-spangled one, and the national anthem is played. Then military jets often fly over the field, signaling the end of the pregame festival. At this point, all heads turn in unison toward home plate as the umpire dons his mask, points at the pitcher, and says: "Play ball!"

Opening Day is about more than pomp and circumstance. As Thomas Boswell put it in an essay titled *Why Time Begins on Opening Day:* "We know that something fine, almost wonderful, is about to begin, but we can't quite say why baseball seems so valuable, almost indispensable, to us. The game, which remains one of our broadest sources of metaphor, changes with our angle of vision, our mood; there seems to be no end to our succession of lucky discoveries. When Opening Day arrives, think how many baseball worlds begin revolving for seven months."

The repeated rituals of Opening Day suggest a "new beginning," an anticipation of the story to be told in the coming season, a story brimming with optimism and hope. And in those months that follow, with the long (but not nearly long enough) march through the dog days of summer, the game is there, day in and day out, in any place marked by the distinct diamond design of a baseball field. And with each ball game, its intricacies, from the double switch to the sacrifice fly to the suicide squeeze, appear in countless combinations—with no two plays ever the same.

Midseason brings a weekend in a Cooperstown, the upstate New York village and mythical but not actual birthplace of the game, where new heroes are elevated to sit alongside those from the past—an enactment of what Eliade called the *Myth of the Eternal Return*, a "revolt against concrete, historical time, their nostalgia for a periodical return to the mythical time of the beginning of things, to the 'Great Time.'"

Autumn brings baseball's high holy days: the post-season and occasionally that holiest of holy days, a seventh game of the World Series, where some of baseball's stories are seared in collective memory.

Among the banners displayed high above center field in the ballpark once known as SkyDome, there is one honoring the 1992 Toronto Blue Jays. That banner commemorates more than a team; it marks and resurrects a singular, trans-formational moment for the franchise, for Canada. Its royal-blue and white trim—the inverse colors of all flags raised to the rafters before it—calls upon fans to look, remember, and return. And just a few feet away hangs a banner bearing the only number retired by the Blue Jays, the number worn by the player whose heroics for Blue Jays fans established that sacred moment in 1992, apart from all others.

It took nine years for the newly created Toronto fran-chise to reach the playoffs (1985). Once this initial success whet fans' appetites for more, they got less: A string of stun-ning pennant race collapses and postseason disappointments began that year and continued for the next six seasons. Leads were lost; great hitters slumped; star pitchers fal-tered: In three playoff series, Toronto's record was a dis-mal 5-12. It was not the Dodgers or Cubs or Red Sox, but for newly initiated Canadians, it was a test of faith.

The 1992 playoffs at first seemed to be a repeat of this theme. In Game Four of the American League Champion-ship Series, the Oakland Athletics took a two-run lead into the top of the ninth inning, with the soon-to-be-named league's Most Valuable Player and Cy Young Award win-ner, Dennis Eckersley, on the mound, poised to even the se-ries at two games apiece. And Toronto fans knew (or thought they knew) where things would go from there.

But with one man on base, Roberto Alomar (in the prime of a Hall of Fame career) connected with a fastball, hitting a line drive toward right field that carried and carried until it finally disappeared over the wall. Images of Alomar barely out of the batter's box, arms raised and index fingers pointing skyward, instantly became the team's defining image. The Blue Jays never looked back, winning the pennant, then the World Series, and doing it again the following year (with slugger Joe Carter playing the role of Bill Mazeroski, hitting a Series-winning home run in Game Six). It was the first time a team had won back-to-back titles since the Yankees in the late seventies.

Alomar's home run did not simply change the narrative; it was a mold breaker, a clue that the future might be different. Its elements are familiar: the heightening of sensitivity that stirs inside the fan during the late innings of an important game, building until the entire season hangs in the balance of a single pitch. There are Toronto fans today who would list that moment in 1992 among the most memorable and satisfying in their lives. So each year as the cycle begins anew, the 1992 banner flies, calling Blue Jays fans to return to that mystical time—*in illo tempore*.

Some sacred moments occur when "time is out" and the game is halted. So it was on September 6, 1995, when the crowd inside Baltimore's Oriole Park at Camden Yards erupted into a twenty-two-minute ovation in honor of Cal Ripken Jr. after the fifth inning in a game against the California Angels.

The game had just then become "official," and it therefore also was official that Ripken had played in his 2,131st consecutive game, breaking what was once thought to be baseball's most unassailable record. As the cheering crowd rose in awe, Ripken circled not the bases but the entire ballpark, stopping frequently to shake hands with fans along the rails. The effect was as magical as it was celebratory. In their book *All Things Shining*, philosophers Hubert Drey-fus and Sean Dorrance Kelly describe how, in such mo-ments, "something overwhelming occurs." As they put it, the cheering crowd "wells up and carries you along as on a powerful wave. The wave metaphor is crucial here. When a wave is at its most powerful, it is a solid foundation that can support as many riders as will fit upon it. It can even sweep up more as it runs along. But when the wave passes, nothing but its memory survives. Try to stand upon the still water and you'll find that the supporting foundation is gone. Those moments of sport are like that. When you are in the midst of them, riding the wave, they carry you along and give meaning to life."

The outpouring of emotion for Ripken was simultane-ously a nod to the quiet dignity of Lou Gehrig, the previous record holder—an example of baseball's intertwining of past and present. The sanctity of Gehrig and his record formed a halo upon Ripken as he broke it; the two were united as one.

It had been almost six decades since Gehrig uttered leg-endary words in his farewell address at Yankee Stadium, a farewell forced by the terminal illness that eventually bore his name: "Today I consider myself the luckiest man on the face of the earth. . . . I might have been given a bad break, but I've got an awful lot to live for." To this day, Gehrig is celebrated on the anniversary of the speech—the Fourth of July—by the Yankees each year they are home (making an already sacred time that much more meaningful), and on one occasion (2009, the seventieth anniversary) by all of baseball, as the speech was recited, word for word, by rep-resentatives of every home team in the major leagues. In this and many other ways, baseball creates and lives the cyclical, repetitive liturgy and sacramental time of religion.

Inti Raymi, the Incan Festival of the Sun, celebrates the winter solstice by honoring the god Inti, with hopes of a good harvest in the coming year. In recent years, the ceremony (their Opening Day) has gained a measure of renown through a historical reconstruction, held in Cusco, Peru, as a weeklong ode to its heritage. But before it was suppressed by the Catholic Church in the sixteenth century, the Inti Raymi was a deeply pious affair and is said to have been marked by precise execution of rituals (some gruesome) in the same manner and location each year. Thousands of Inca convened, often after journeying hundreds of miles, usually on foot, in the hope of touching a higher spiritual plane while reliving their mythical story of origin, together. And over millennia, such sacramental moments have been part of humankind's effort to touch the deepest plane of existence. This is the power of myth.

Today, especially in the West, that word, *myth,* too often is used as a synonym for falsehood. The Greek word *mythos* originally meant a truth that is experienced, an awareness that lies beyond words. As theologian Karen Armstrong wrote, "A myth was never intended as an accurate account of a historical event; it was *something that had in some sense happened once but that also happens all the time.*"

Mythos takes us to sacred places and sacred times—spaces and times beyond. To places revered for their mystical power, evoking an ineffable feeling of connection to something greater like Newgrange, Stonehenge, Uluru, and Easter Island. And to sacred times like Easter, Yom Kippur, Ramadan, and the Inti Raymi festival, or to a ball field on Opening Day.

In the decades since C. P. Snow decried the split between science and religion in his seminal lecture, *The Two Cultures,* the chasm between the two has widened. Today, skeptics often use science to mock religion, typically by dismissing the anthropomorphic God of the simplest forms of theism. And sometimes they dismiss the religious dimension altogether. This is a mistake. In fact, we humans can go beyond science even as we embrace it and its wonderful gifts.

Albert Einstein once said: "As the circle of light increases, so does the circumference of darkness around it." Sometimes that darkness awaits additional light, light that will transform the unknown into the known. But sometimes, as Einstein himself attested, the darkness represents the unknowable, the ineffable. Thus, the transcendentalist Henry David Thoreau wrote in his journal on Christmas Day, 1851:

> I, standing twenty miles off, see a crimson cloud in the horizon. You tell me it is a mass of vapor which absorbs all other rays and reflects the red, but that is nothing to the purpose, for this red vision excites me, stirs my blood, makes my thoughts flow, and I have new and indescribable fancies, and you have not touched the secret of that influence. If there is not something mystical in your explanation, something unexplainable to the understanding, some elements of mystery, it is quite insufficient. If there is nothing in it which speaks to my imagination, what boots it? What sort of science is that which enriches the understanding, but robs the imagination?

Thoreau was pointing to Rudolf Otto's *mysterium tremendum et fascinans*. Meaning can be found beyond what we can capture rationally (including what we capture in the dogmatic trappings of religion), whether it is evoked by music, art, or nature.

Or baseball.

It was just one short phrase, possibly uttered in jest, but it came to epitomize as improbable a season as there has ever been in the major leagues. "Ya gotta believe" was what relief pitcher Tug McGraw yelled at his New York Mets teammates early in July of 1973.

The Mets had little to sustain them at the time, mired as they were at the bottom of their division in the National League, well below .500. They seemed a mediocre team in a crowded, mediocre division, distinguished only by their marvelous pitching (anchored by starters Tom Seaver, Jon Matlack, and Jerry Koosman and by a bullpen led by the suddenly blooming, if odd, McGraw); they did at least have a bit of nostalgia about them (with Willie Mays returning to New York to play his final season, and with Yogi Berra having come crosstown to manage the hapless team). On offense, they were batting a hideous .238.

But a month later, as they started to make their move,

McGraw's exclamation became a rallying cry, first for the team, then for all New York.

On September 21, the Mets, sporting a .500 record, stumbled into first place; and they went on to win their division with only three more victories than defeats. Then, miraculously, they beat the nascent Big Red Machine in Cincinnati to get into the World Series with what remains the lowest winning percentage in major league history. Only a loss in Game Seven to the mighty Oakland Athletics kept them from a world championship.

On that day in July when something moved McGraw to speak, the team's lousy record had prompted a clubhouse lecture from board chairman M. Donald Grant, which the irrepressible McGraw interrupted with his shout. Having done so, he was so worried that Grant might think he was mocking the owner's rah-rah rant that he spoke to the boss afterward to assure him he was serious.

Sincere or not, "Ya gotta believe" survives in baseball lore because it was just about all the team had. If there is a case for the importance of what are called intangibles in baseball, the 1973 Mets are prime evidence.

Baseball is a game of infinite variation and possibility. As Bob Lemon of the Cleveland Indians observed after he had stopped playing and started managing, "I don't care how long you've been around, you'll never see it all." So faith that the seemingly impossible might occur is part of the game.

Faith does not have to be loud or full of swagger, as it was for McGraw. It often is private. It can be bestowed by a parent or it can be acquired one element at a time. It can come in a flash or very slowly, even painfully. And faith is not certainty; it is a special kind of confidence.

A leap of faith, after all, is an embrace of feeling over logic, a willingness to loosen one's dependence on the purely rational. Thomas Aquinas said, "To one who has faith, no explanation is necessary. To one without faith, no explanation is possible." That is because faith is anchored in deeply personal, experienced truths. The theologian Karen Armstrong wrote that "one of the conditions of enlightenment has always been a willingness to let go of what we thought we knew in order to appreciate truths we had never dreamed of"—an opening of oneself to mystery.

Aaron Boone, who with one swing of his bat in 2003 became a legend, had acquired faith—and fed the faith of others. The scion of a Major League Baseball dynasty (grandson of Ray, son of Bob, and brother of Bret), he had come to the New York Yankees in the middle of the season from Cincinnati after several modestly successful years, but had left no discernible mark in his short time wearing pinstripes until he was inserted as a pinch runner into Game Seven of the American League Championship Series against the archrival Boston Red Sox. Boone came in to run for pinch hitter Ruben Sierra in the eighth inning following a dramatic three-run Yankee rally that exploited one of the worst managerial decisions ever (by Grady Little of the Red Sox, who left an aging and tired Pedro Martinez in for one inning too many). Boone stayed in the game at third base as it went into extra innings and was due to lead off the Yankee half of the eleventh.

By then, the Yankee bullpen was spent. Mariano Rivera had just finished his third and final inning, and the Bombers (a nickname that stuck from the record-shattering Ruth–Gehrig era) needed to end the game quickly. By his own account, facing a skilled knuckleball thrower in Tim Wakefield, Boone was prepared to take Wakefield's first pitch in order to get a feel for his tricky delivery. However, as Boone waited on deck for Wakefield to complete his warm-up tosses, Derek Jeter, already one of the Yankees' living legends, approached him. Sensing Boone's tension, Jeter told him not to worry: "The ghosts will come."

Jeter was referring not to the famous Curse that had, so the legend goes, kept the Red Sox from a world championship since 1918; he was referring to all the legendary figures of the Yankees' unmatched, celebrated past (Ruth, Gehrig, DiMaggio, Mantle) who had helped put the Yankees in thirty-eight of the first ninety-eight World Series and who had enabled them to win twenty-six of them. In a flash, Boone's attitude changed. As he walked to home plate, he junked his plan to take the first pitch. Instead, he would be looking for what the players call "a pitch to hit."

Wakefield obliged with a knuckleball that didn't flutter very much and drifted toward the middle of the plate. Boone was ready and sent a beautiful, long fly ball deep into the left field grandstand. Bedlam ensued. Jeter's message had transformed Boone from a defensive hitter to an aggressive one, the kind who wins pennants. His faith had carried him forward.

So it was with another monumental home run. This one, hit in the 1988 World Series, may be the most exciting mixture of spirit, mind, and matter in the history of the game.

Kirk Gibson was one of those stars about whom managers dream. He could run like the wind, hit for power, field his outfield positions with acrobatic skill, and motivate his teammates with his hustle and fierce competitiveness. He came first to the Detroit Tigers after an All-American career at Michigan State University in two sports (the NFL coveted him as a wide receiver); soon he emerged as a key cog in their 1984 championship season.

As a Dodger in 1988, Gibson had a Most Valuable Player season and led the team through a tough seven-game National League Championship Series against the Mets. But he was a wreck on the eve of Game One of an intra-California World Series battle with the heavily favored Oakland Athletics. He had a damaged left hamstring and a severely injured right knee; moreover, on the day of the fateful game, he had developed a stomach virus. He was nursing his wounds and missing from the Dodger dugout as the game began— nestled in the adjacent clubhouse, listening to NBC's broadcasters declaring him unfit to play.

However, Dodger manager Tommy Lasorda refused to accept his star's total absence. Lasorda loved players who hustled and delivered in the clutch. He was desperate to get Gibson into the game, even if only for a pinch-hitting appearance, both for his potential impact on the outcome and his certain impact on the team's spirit. Between innings, he regularly stuck his head in the clubhouse door to ask his star if he thought he could hit; each time, though, Gibson glumly gave a thumbs-down response.

Until the ninth inning. With the A's nursing a 4–3 lead, the Dodgers were facing the best relief pitcher in the game, Dennis Eckersley. Originally a flashy starter with Cleveland and Boston, Eckersley had matured (achieving sobriety along the way) into a dominating closer, with forty-five saves to his credit that year alone—although he was destined for agony on this night and four years later against Roberto Alomar.

In the clubhouse, before the Dodgers came to bat in the bottom of the ninth, Gibson realized that the pitcher's spot was due up fourth, which meant the Dodgers might need a pinch hitter. He dispatched a message to Lasorda that he would try to hit, and he returned to a batting tee set up in the room for practice swings. He groaned in pain with every swing.

Meanwhile, Eckersley appeared headed for yet another save, getting two quick outs as Gibson limped into the dugout. Before he could climb the steps, however, Lasorda ordered him to stop. The crafty manager did not want Gibson in the on-deck circle as the third Dodger hitter of the inning, outfielder Mike Davis, walked to home plate; he wanted everyone, above all Eckersley, to see a light-hitting reserve infielder, Dave Anderson, on deck. Because Davis had hit for power the previous three seasons while playing for Oakland, the Dodger manager was certain Eckersley would pitch to him carefully with an easier out on deck. Eckersley did, walking him. And Gibson got his chance.

The Dodger Stadium crowd roared as Gibson limped toward home plate.

Eckersley pitched masterfully—inside and outside, high and low. He missed with a couple after Gibson fouled off three, his intense pain obvious to everyone. On a 2-2 pitch, with Eckersley's concentration completely on Gibson, Davis stole second base on ball three (shades of the Dave Roberts's play against the Yankees sixteen years later), meaning that a mere single could tie the game.

Eckersley was preparing to throw the payoff pitch when Gibson suddenly called time and stepped out of the batter's box. To the naked eye, his deep breath signaled a final effort to compose himself and concentrate. However, as Gibson later revealed, he was thinking about the scouting report on the A's before the Series began. It had been compiled by one of those characters who make baseball so endearing, a sharp-eyed man from Louisiana, Mel Didier, then sixty years old, who had spent his career finding, helping develop, and scouting major league talent.

Throughout baseball, Eckersley was known for his devilish slider, a particularly tricky pitch to hit. If it is thrown correctly (the grip should be on the outer third of the baseball instead of over the middle), it will move, or "slide," laterally as well as down. Encountering a group of the Dodgers' left-handed hitters before the Series (a small bunch that included Mike Scioscia and switch hitter John "T-Bone" Shelby), Didier delivered this oracular message: With a full count, a lefty could count on what baseball people call a "backdoor slider"—for them it would move down and toward the inside corner if thrown perfectly. Gibson resolved to bet on a slider and focused on swinging low, his best chance to put the thick, or fat, part of his bat on the ball, with what he liked to call his "emergency stroke."

True to form, Eckersley threw the backdoor slider and Gibson connected solidly, his healthy upper body providing all of the power through his swing. The Dodgers' renowned broadcaster, Vin Scully, barely had time to announce a fly ball to right field before the ball landed deep in the seats. There is no more famous World Series image than the sight of an overjoyed Gibson rounding second base, pumping his right arm repeatedly as he limped toward home. After a momentary pause that allowed the home viewers to absorb the moment, Scully serenaded them with what is now among baseball's most memorable calls: "In a season that has been so improbable, the impossible has happened!"

This was faith in action: Lasorda's belief in his star and Gibson's faith in himself, supplemented by a healthy dose of detailed preparation.

Faith is often the handmaiden of hard work, intellectual and otherwise. In religion, thinkers often have tried to use reason to convince others to join them in faith. Much ink has been spilled, for example, on various philosophical arguments designed to "prove" God's existence. I find it interesting that the argumentative style and logical structure of some of these arguments have parallels in baseball that could be used—with equal force—to suggest that something more than coincidence is involved in some of baseball's most delightful anomalies.

Consider, for example, this piece of trivia. The annual MVP (Most Valuable Player) Award has existed in its modern form since 1931. A few remarkable players have won the award not just once, and not just more than once, but two years in a row. Wondrously (miraculously?), the first nine men to win the award back-to-back could fill the nine spots on a lineup card: that is, at the start of their MVP years, each of the nine played one of the nine positions in the field (one at first base, one at second, one at short, and so on—no two the same).

THE BALLPLAYERS WITH THEIR
POSITIONS, TEAMS, AND MVP YEARS

◆

Pitcher: Hal Newhouser of the Detroit Tigers (1944 and 1945)

Catcher: Yogi Berra of the New York Yankees (1954 and 1955)

First base: Jimmie Foxx of the Philadelphia Athletics (1932 and 1933)

Second base: Joe Morgan of the Cincinnati Reds (1975 and 1976)

Shortstop: Ernie Banks of the Chicago Cubs (1958 and 1959)

Third base: Mike Schmidt of the Philadelphia Phillies (1980 and 1981)

Left field: Dale Murphy of the Atlanta Braves (1982 and 1983)

Center field: Mickey Mantle of the Yankees (1956 and 1957)

Right field: Roger Maris of the Yankees (1960 and 1961)

This wonderful list allows believers in the specialness of baseball to say "such things don't just happen." This is an intellectual cousin of a common argument for the existence of God, an argument that has been employed by various faithful since it was first used by the ancient Greeks, a backdoor contention that the delicate, ordered, intricate mosaic of the universe could not exist without a higher intelligent force doing the ordering. In short, the nature of nature proves there is a creator-God.

This clock-maker argument (as it often is called)—that a timepiece, with all its intricate interconnected parts, presumes a clock-maker/creator's design—is to some the basis of faith. For most, the clock-maker argument proves no more than the MVP data: It is interesting, but not dispositive. Faith, not reason, gets us to God. As Rabbi Heschel said of the clock-maker argument: "The problem thus faced concerns not the existence of the universe but its cause; not its present but its past. Since the ultimate structure and order of nature were thought of in mechanical terms, its origin or creation was also conceived of as a mechanical process, comparable to the process of constructing a watch. The shortcomings of this view lie in its taking both the watch and all of reality for granted." What is more, Heschel said, "The moment we utter the name of God we leave the level of scientific thinking and enter the realm of the ineffable."

I don't believe that a clock-maker directed the Mets' drive to a pennant in 1973, or that any ghosts were present as the drama of the 2003 Red Sox–Yankee playoff built toward Aaron Boone's decision not to take Tim Wakefield's first pitch, or that there was an invisible hand guiding either Tommy Lasorda's determination to play Kirk Gibson in 1988 or Gibson's sudden recollection of the scouting report on Dennis Eckersley's backdoor slider.

But baseball offers a window into the nature of faith, even in the deepest meanings of the word—as a source of comfort, of motivation, of understanding, and above all, of meaning and ultimate purpose. There are moments when baseball can lift us from the ordinary to a different plane as well as propel a drive toward a National League pennant. Tug McGraw had it: Ya gotta believe.

For this reason, I take baseball seriously—at a profound level. For me it is also very personal.

As it happens, Tug McGraw and his teammates knew a little something about winning in unlikely situations. Four years earlier, in a season so stunningly improbable that the word *miracle* has always been attached to it, the Mets, up to then the lowliest of teams, found a way to win the World Series. But for me, the Mets' unexpected rise forced a personal question: Which team should I bestow upon my son, Jed, who was born in January of that same year, 1969? Baseball fandom, like religion, after all, is most often a matter of legacy; it is something inherited and passed on from one generation to the next. In the words of popular science writer Chet Raymo: "People who hold religious beliefs . . . seldom consider, for example, that the factor that correlates most closely with their beliefs is the circumstance of their birth. The vast majority of Christians were born Christians; the vast majority of Muslims were born Muslims." In this sense, the vast majority of Angels and Cubs fans were born that way as well.

Of course, legacy is not the sole reason why a person prays to a certain deity or roots for a certain team, but for most people, it's how it starts. And I knew that the team I chose for Jed was likely to stay with him for life—perhaps longer than the Catholicism I bestowed upon him by having him baptized.

Tommy Lasorda has described his relationship to the Dodgers as devout, something that stirs deep inside his core, which he calls "bleeding Dodger blue." For many years, I had been Lasorda, bleeding Dodger blue from birth. But in 1969, I was forced to reconsider. And I knew I could not impose my Dodgers upon Jed; they only came to town for six games a year and their contests were usually decided too late in California to make the morning papers. The choice reduced to the Yankees (the nemesis of my youth) and the Miracle Mets. The difference between the two teams, in terms of quality and personality, couldn't have been any starker.

The Yankees of 1969 were pitiful. It had been only five seasons since the team's five consecutive American League titles, but the halcyon days of Mickey Mantle and Roger Maris seemed like a very distant memory. In the half decade since, they had lost 424 games; only the Athletics, the Senators, and the Angels had lost more in the American League.

Yankees fans, having grown accustomed to pennants and parades, were stunned. Mickey Mantle, the last of the old, great Yanks, retired before the 1969 season. It is telling that the most dramatic thing to happen to those 1969 Yankees was that shortstop (later a general manager) Gene Michael succeeded in pulling the hidden ball trick—a ruse usually unseen beyond Little League—and for good measure, he did it four other times in his career. There were two pitchers on the team, lefties Fritz Peterson and Mike Kekich, who later gained a measure of fame, or infamy, for swapping their wives and entire families (dogs included), leading one Yankee executive to quip, "We may have to call off family day."

Bizarre, yes, but more than that, the story helped form a collage that depicted Yankees' dysfunction—just how far the once mighty team had gone astray in recent years—and more than any other example, it encapsulated the period that the Yankees spent wandering baseball's wilderness. Salvation, spurred by a shipping magnate named Steinbrenner, was still another four years away.

The Mets, meanwhile, were captivating the city, win by

unlikely win, all the way to the World Series. But to me, the expansion team, then in its eighth season, didn't possess sufficient gravitas and did not touch the soul as had the Dodgers, even if Brooklyn stalwart Gil Hodges was flashing signs as the manager from their dugout and their uniform featured Dodger blue in a nod to the team that had once played in Brooklyn. Simply put, the Mets would have been the easy choice, but they didn't speak to the depths of the "fifties Catholic" in me—the part that responds to Tradition with a capital *T*. The Yankees, despite their recent troubles, had both gravitas and Tradition.

Those who are taught to see the world through the lens of religion think in the long term. Faith goes century by century. And as a professor and chairman of the religion department at St. Francis College in Brooklyn at the time, I tried to practice what I preached. The Yankees were sure to return to form eventually, or so I figured. The Mets were the moment; the Yankees were enduring tradition.

And giving my son the Yankees would also be giving him the trappings of their history, from the larger-than-life persona of Babe Ruth to the gracefulness of Lou Gehrig to the elegance of Joe DiMaggio—all that Jeter (at this point, a gleam in his parents' eyes) later invoked to Boone as he stepped toward the batter's box that October night in 2003, the ghosts.

But I also realized that picking the Yankees, the team that tormented me for much of my youth, would be an act of self-sacrifice—one that might seem trivial to the uninitiated, but one that a fervent fan would recognize as borderline sacrilegious.

These were the thoughts racing through my head when I faced the moment of truth—when I decided to give Jed the Yankees. Gravitas and Tradition, a fitting gift. Ultimately, my decision rested on one factor and one factor alone: the love between father and son.

It was a decision that I did not come to lightly. In the sixties, Catholicism was undergoing the tremendous transformation from being a triumphalist religion to an ecumenical one, a wondrous embrace of all perspectives led by a great pope, John XXIII. There was turbulence in and around established orders—religious, political, and otherwise—the beginning of the decline in faith in institutions we see today. Could baseball and its teams be the exception? Could we still believe in them? I at least wanted to give my son a chance at saying yes and at having a tradition to enjoy.

Of course in my own life, I had experienced by this point the wrenching of the Dodgers from their rightful place—the theft of the team by Walter O'Malley, as if he and not the people of Brooklyn owned them. But this only underscored for me the important role baseball can play from childhood to old age. Just as I had once forged a powerful bond with my father through a ball club, so too, I decided, must my son be given the opportunity to experience such wonders with me.

Here, there is an interesting twist (in a way, a twist of the knife). For sure, my father had given me the Dodgers; but he also played a role in ushering in the O'Malley era. A Brooklyn political figure, he was among those who initially recommended a young O'Malley to the Dodgers after team officials sought his advice on hiring a new attorney. Thus was set in motion a chain of events I would later describe hyperbolically to my friends, "My father is responsible for the removal of the Dodgers from Brooklyn." In a sense, by causing the delivery of my son into the ranks of the Yankee faithful, I carried on the Sexton tradition of betraying the Dodgers. I eventually compounded the sin by becoming a Yankees fan myself. In religion, we call this conversion.

In the decades since that moment of truth, Jed, who was baptized, has been bar mitzvahed; he is Jewish today, the faith of my wife, our daughter, our daughter-in-law, and our three granddaughters (my Irish Catholic brother-in-law, my sister's husband, likes to joke that "not since Abraham left Ur has a gentile begat as many Jews as John"). But the baseball faith that I conferred to my son has remained a constant throughout his entire life. He still roots for the New York Yankees.

Jed's faith was once a gift, or at least a bequest, from me. So it is for the vast majority of believers initially. What someone does with that gift, of course, is one of the central challenges of any life. A religious tradition, as well as love for a baseball team, must, as time passes, be tested and thus doubted. At some point reaffirmation is required. In some Christian traditions, this is what is meant by being born again; in others, particularly in the East, it is the very process of reexamination that is revered, especially in traditions where the uncritical acceptance of anything is seen as unworthy.

In that spirit, as I began life as a professor of religion at St. Francis College, a Catholic school for commuter students from working-class families, I told a story one day in the fall of 1968. It was the kind of story they might have heard learning folk religion in the Catholic elementary and secondary schools; I was working hard to wean them from the simple pieties and blind acceptance of all that in order to experience the study of religion as an intellectual exercise— a real college course. My story was intended to be demonstrably false. And my strategy was to use the revelation of its falsehood in the next class (one week later) as a springboard for a discussion of the true nature of religion, misplaced certitude, and the power of true faith.

It was the day of Game Five in the World Series between the Tigers and Cardinals, with St. Louis ahead three games to one and most fans believing the Series was all but over. But I told my students that I knew better. The Lady of Fatima had appeared before me the night before and predicted that Detroit would come back and beat the Cardinals. Naturally, they were skeptical. But incredibly, led by a portly, hypercompetitive pitcher, Mickey Lolich, the Tigers did precisely that—beating the Cardinals' incomparable Bob Gibson in the seventh game.

The following week, the students posted a copy of that week's betting line for the upcoming National Football League games on the blackboard; they wanted to know what the Lady of Fatima had told me about the games. So I told them that she had appeared to me and given two more messages: one, that gambling was a sin; and two, that the then-mediocre New York Jets would go on to win Super Bowl III. Little did anyone—least of all me—expect what Joe Namath would do that January.

I doubt I was taken literally by any of my students, but the legend started to grow: Fatima speaks to Sexton. My lesson had failed, in no small part because the pull of the Fatima story remains so powerful. It is based on an account by three young people in 1917 of an appearance by Mary in rural Portugal six times that year, during which three messages were given in secret and eventually written down by one of the children who later became a nun, Lucia Santos. Two of them were made public during World War II, with the third not released until nearly sixty years later.

In popular retelling, it is often said that the secrets involved prophecies (eventually validated) about World War I and II, and even the assassination attempts on Pope John Paul II. In fact, the sister's accounts are quite mystical in tone and not particularly specific with regard to future events, more allegory than prophecy. My very rare predictive success more than forty years ago was merely that; the Holy Mother played no role.

The result of one's spiritual journey and the reflection it entails is more consequential than such blind faith and more profound even than the hope born out of necessity that Tug McGraw and his teammates found when their backs were against the wall. At its best, a reflection upon one's faith can reveal what Paul Tillich called "the ultimate concern," that which motivates people day in and day out, perhaps leading to the complete emptying of self, as seen for example in a Buddhist monk.

Whatever its particular manifestation, faith is an affirmation of something that cannot be expressed, for it is rooted in another domain of knowledge, one that is beyond what is knowable in scientific terms. There is much that is known today, and even more that is unknown today but will be known (perhaps even hundreds of years from now). Faith— true faith—deals with neither the known nor the unknown but knowable. It deals with that which is unknowable in the scientific sense but which the believer knows with all of his or her being (the way, in a wonderful marriage, love is known). This is the domain of faith. Therein lies the most powerful connection to baseball, its rhythms and patterns, astonishing feats and mystical charm; it is not necessary to elevate baseball to the level of ultimate concern to notice that, for the true fan, there is sometimes a touching of the ineffable that displays the qualities of a religious experience in the profound space of faith.

As Ralph Waldo Emerson put it, "All I have seen teaches me to trust the Creator for all I have not seen." That thought was echoed by William James: "The divine presence is known through experience. The turning to a higher plane is a distinct act of consciousness. It is not a vague, twilight or semi-conscious experience," he wrote. "It is not a trance."

And psychiatrist Emanuel Tanay, a Holocaust survivor, also tells us that faith can spur feelings of confidence and optimism: "As your faith is strengthened you will find that . . . things will flow as they will, and that you will flow with them, to your great delight and benefit."

It took only a moment, but Derek Jeter's words about the Yankee ghosts reached Aaron Boone with a sudden clarity that autumn night; delight and benefit followed.

He didn't "gotta," but he believed.

THIRD INNING
Doubt

In 1966, the Boston Red Sox managed to lose ninety baseball games, one more than the then-floundering New York Yankees and more than any other team in the American League. That miserable performance climaxed more than a decade of decline and disappointment, and as far as the team and its fans were concerned, the past appeared likely to be but prologue.

They did have a new manager in 1967, a former Red Sox player named Dick Williams. But the most he could promise was that the team, with a few new faces, would never stop hustling. And in a pledge that trumpeted its own limitations, Williams vowed that the team "will win more than we lose." Sox fans were unconvinced. On Opening Day, a paltry 8,324 came to Fenway Park, the smallest crowd to see a home opener in fourteen years.

But the team actually began the season the way Williams had promised, and game by improbable game the fans' perceptions of the Red Sox and the team's perception of its own capabilities began to change. They somehow survived the loss of a brilliant, young slugging outfielder, Tony Conigliaro, to a hideous beaning in August. And six weeks later—on the final day of the season no less—they won a four-way pennant race to produce the town's first American League title in twenty-one years.

That amazing turnaround season, which ended just one game short of a world championship when the Sox lost to the St. Louis Cardinals, was appropriately dubbed the Impossible Dream (*Man of La Mancha* was the hot Broadway musical then); it took only one season of hope (after the deep doubts built over fifteen years of failure) to change the atmosphere around Fenway Park utterly.

The same thing happened in New York two years later. For the fledgling New York Mets, 1968 represented another year of miserable (though occasionally entertaining) baseball. They lost eighty-nine games; only the Houston Astros lost more (one more), in the entire National League. The Mets had finished last or next to last in the ten-team league each year of their existence.

Their 1969 comeback was different from the steady climb of the Red Sox in 1967. For the first third of the season, the Mets were better—but they were barely winning more than they were losing. What made the Mets "Amazin' " were their winning streaks—eleven here, ten there. By Labor Day, they found themselves in contention for the pennant with the Chicago Cubs.

"It built in such an improbable way," said their popular right fielder Ron Swoboda, a decent hitter but a famously poor fielder (who nonetheless would make two spectacular run-saving catches in the World Series that fall). Reflecting the absence of optimism (the absence of faith) that flows from deep doubts grounded in experience, Swoboda said years later: "In 1969, I thought we would take the next step forward. I thought we'd be a little better than we were in '68, around .500, a little above, a little below."

He was wrong. When a fly ball hit by Baltimore's Davey Johnson settled in the glove of left fielder Cleon Jones, the Mets (who had won a hundred games during the regular season) were champions of the world.

Strictly as baseball, the '67 Red Sox and '69 Mets make some sense. They each had a core of younger players and rookies who did not share the institutional memory of lousy seasons. The doubts about each team as their turnaround seasons began were probably excessive.

But to the ballplayers and their fans, the two seasons were much more magical. In each case, the season began with fans doubting that they could win, ever. It was logical, fact-based doubt and it arose from considerable, painful experience. The teams had no expectations that the coming season would be appreciably different from the previous one, although their professional duty was to try nonetheless. Only after an unpredictable number of victories in single games did the players' outlook, imperceptibly at first, start to move from doubt to hope and even faith, as they began to say, "We can do this." Their faith was confirmed by what they were experiencing on the field—some would call it a miracle or gift—and experience overcame doubt. To theologians, this is a familiar process.

Doubt is at the core of baseball, touching every player and every fan. And doubt is central to the religious experience. They are not separate, they coexist. In baseball as in religion, doubt and faith are intertwined.

Some see doubt as the enemy of faith. The fifteen-volume Catholic Encyclopedia presents *doubt* and *faith* as antonyms, morally as well as literally, stating flatly that they cannot coexist: "It follows that doubt in regard to the Christian religion is equivalent to its total rejection."

But through the ages, while some have seen doubt in this

way, many have not. Saint Augustine, early in the first millennium, wrote that "doubt is but another element of faith." And sixteen centuries later, the theologian Paul Tillich wrote: "The doubt which is implicit in every act of faith is neither the methodological nor the skeptical doubt . . . it is the doubt of him who is ultimately concerned about a concrete content. One could call it the existential doubt, in contrast to the methodological and the skeptical doubt. It does not question whether a special proposition is true or false. It does not reject every concrete truth, but it is aware of the element of insecurity in every existential truth." This type of doubt, he said, is implied in faith. The two concepts are the complementary ends of a tuning fork. The poet Robert Browning put it well: "You call for faith: I show you doubt, to prove that faith exists. The more of doubt, the stronger faith, I say, if faith o'ercomes doubt."

The ancient traditions of the East have long taught: "Great doubt, great awakening; little doubt, little awakening; no doubt, no awakening." The Mahabharata, the Indian epic almost ten times longer than the *Iliad* and *Odyssey* combined, is the story of a family feud between the Pandavas and Kauravas that ends in a horrific war. The Pandavas have been cheated out of their kingdom, have seen one of their female members, Draupadi, defiled in public, have wandered in the forests for twelve years, and have now returned to recover their lands in a bargain with their rivals. But the Kauravas renege, setting the stage for the epic battle. With thousands of war elephants and war chariots ready to go and conches trumpeting the advent of the fight, Arjuna, a prince of the Pandavas, has his charioteer drive him to the center of the battlefield. Looking at his relatives and their allies (including some of his former teachers) across the field, Arjuna has doubts—not about his ability as Kshatriya, or warrior, but about the morality of his undertaking. He sets aside his bow and declares that he will not fight his

family and teachers because it is against his religious training to do so.

Arjuna's charioteer is the god Krishna, and over the next
eighty pages of the epic, Krishna persuades Arjuna that it is
his duty to fight. This story, initiated by Arjuna's doubt, is
known as the Bhagavad Gita, by itself one of the world's
great spiritual books. Interestingly, if ironically, to help himself through some doubting moments that plagued even
him, the pacifist Mahatma Gandhi carried with him a copy
of this story of war.

Doubt, in other words, is neither limited by geography
nor sectarian dogma; the faithful live with doubt, saints
included. Mother Teresa of Calcutta, in one of the letters
published after her death, wrote openly of her doubt: "Jesus has a very special love for you. As for me, the silence and
the emptiness is so great that I look and do not see, listen
and do not hear."

Even Christ had doubts. In the Gospel of Matthew, as
his crucifixion drew near, Jesus fell to the ground and said,
"My Father, if it be possible, let this cup pass from me;
nevertheless, not as I will, but as you will."

And the Apostle Thomas (through the years since known
as both Doubting Thomas and Thomas the Believer) famously doubted his leader following the resurrection.

The faith that confronts such doubt is not the same
thing as certitude. It goes beyond reason and resists reduc-
ing the world to our terms, categories, and propositions. As
Rabbi Heschel observed: "This does not reflect a process of
thinking that is neatly arranged in the order of doubt first
and faith second; first the question, then the answer. It reflects a situation in which the mind stands *face to face* with
the mystery rather than its own concepts." Faith and doubt,
in religion and in baseball, are companions.

This eternally vexing topic was on the mind of a wise,
if fictional, priest from the Yankees' neighborhood, the

Bronx, as he began to speak at Sunday mass. "Doubt can be a bond as powerful and sustaining as certainty," Father Brendan Flynn, a central character in a riveting Pulitzer Prize–winning play by John Patrick Shanley, *Doubt: A Parable*, explains from the pulpit of his parish. Accused of child abuse by a determined nun who was *certain* he was guilty, his intense byplay with her is unsettlingly provocative, illustrating the dangers of certainty and the role of doubt.

The character's words still resonated in my head when I held a dinner for Shanley (an NYU graduate) after *Doubt* won the Tony Award for Best Play. The gathering was intimate, no more than twenty people, many of whom wanted to know if Hollywood had come knocking (it had) and whether Shanley planned to once again occupy the director's chair after a film absence of nearly two decades (he did, for Meryl Streep no less). But I was more interested in the story he had just finished telling, which illustrated that doubt is no enemy of faith.

As I remember Shanley telling it, the muse that inspired the play was none other than the tough Bronx streets of his youth. It's no coincidence that Father Flynn's church is set in the very same place. In this side story, Shanley was around thirteen years old and already knew his friends were rough and capable of teenage cruelty. But what he witnessed, repeatedly, was the most horrible of cruelties. So much so that he still carries the images with him today.

Shanley's friends would often surround a neighborhood kid, let's call him Louie, who at the age of eighteen had contracted polio and was confined to a wheelchair. They would poke his legs with sticks; then they would taunt him, call him names like "cripple" and "gimp." The teenagers would even make fun of Louie's arms, which grew disproportionately large from navigating his wheelchair around the crowded city streets every day. "Come on," they'd say after prodding him. "If you're so strong, why can't you catch us?" The indignity went on for another eight years.

That's when Louie, now twenty-six, after one more jab in the leg, sprang from his wheelchair, ran down the block, tackled his assailant, and delivered blow after blow until the astonished onlookers gathered enough of their senses to peel Louie off his now bloodied former tormentor.

It was a painstakingly orchestrated charade, perpetuated over his eight years of military eligibility and designed to keep Louie out of the draft and nine thousand miles from the jungles of Vietnam. "I knew I could never tell the good guys from the bad guys again," Shanley said, revealing the source of *Doubt*.

For more than a year, this story stayed with me. Then one May, when Shanley and I were together for the processional walk at the university's commencement ceremony in Yankee Stadium, where I would present him with an honorary degree, I pulled him aside. "John, I'm just haunted by that story," I said. "But it occurs to me, I don't know if it's true." Shanley looked at me, paused, and simply said, "You never will." I let it rest there, even though I could have pressed him and he would have told me.

Each of us consciously or unconsciously decides how much doubt we will tolerate; sometimes there is a delight to maintaining doubt, even where we could choose certitude. On occasion, I myself have made this choice.

In 2001, just after I was named NYU's president, I received a package from *The New York Times*. The short note with it read: *We know that you're a huge fan of baseball and of Jackie Robinson in particular, so as a special memento we are presenting you from our archives this original 1955 Jackie Robinson glove.* I read the words four times: *This original 1955 Jackie Robinson glove.*

It had been forty-six years since Robinson helped Brooklyn to its only World Series win, but despite the passage of time, he has endured as my hero. I am beyond proud that his magnificent wife, Rachel, has an advanced degree from NYU (in nursing) and that I can count her as a friend (I carry with me, as a testament to marital love, a wonderful picture of an older Jackie, his head lovingly resting on Rachel's shoulder). I had Jackie's number 42 sewn in the cuff on my academic gown (possibly in penance for getting my chipped tooth repaired), paying tribute to him in much the same way that Major League Baseball did when it ruled that no new player would ever again wear 42—except for each April 15, the anniversary of his first game in the majors, when every player wears it.

But then it struck me. Maybe this wasn't *Jackie's* glove. Maybe it was just a Jackie Robinson *model* glove, similar to gloves carrying baseball players' names that stores have been offering for years. Was this glove actually used by my hero or did it once sit on a sales rack at Sears? I read the letter again; it was delphic, capable of either interpretation.

Over the years, I've discovered in conversations with friends that some people, faced with such a situation, would call the newspaper to clarify the language; others wouldn't. Interestingly, a dinner with some curators at the British Museum revealed that *none* of them, all folks whose lives are devoted to authenticating works of art, would make such a call. In my mind, the choice was clear. I was glad to embrace the possibility, however remote, that this glove actually was worn by Jackie, at least once, on the green fields of my youth.

I recognize that by making this decision, I reveal a certain unbecoming willingness to forswear available knowledge, since whether it was actually a glove Jackie used was unknown to me but knowable (as opposed to being unknowable like the deepest matters of faith and doubt). I stand convicted in this case, though I hope, on this rare occasion, I will be forgiven for choosing a certain connection (however unproven or ambiguous) to the great Robinson over possible disappointment. My forbearance in the search for truth also displays some of the unhealthy mental characteristics of those who refuse to accept the revelations of carbon dating in order to live in comfortable belief that the world was created in seven, twenty-four-hour days. On such matters, I abandon my tolerance for ambiguity. It usually is the case that, where doubt can be resolved, it should be. Rare—and cherished—are those instances in which the only answer for doubt is faith.

Whatever one's tolerance for ambiguity, however, religion is replete with the interplay of faith and doubt, whether the subject is icons or relics or parables or the most fundamental elements of faith. And often the truth affirmed by faith does not depend upon the factual accuracy of the verbal account that carries the message. For many believers, for example, it is beside the point whether the Bible's account of the Good Samaritan is literally true; what counts is the lesson it conveys. So also the story of Lazarus's rising from the dead or even the resurrection or the provenance of the Shroud of Turin.

For those whose faith derives from the literal truth of these accounts, the stories and objects obviously have immense power; but the point is that the stories can resonate even for those who do not see them as literal accounts but see them as myths capturing a truth beyond. For those in the latter group, they are hierophanies, pathways to a deep truth. For both groups, however, doubt plays a role: For those who take the stories literally, doubt is a deep threat, potentially causing the story to unravel if contrary facts are shown. And for those for whom the story is a pathway to an ineffable truth beyond, doubt is the reminder to be humble as one confronts the unknowable through faith, never assuming one has a complete and final understanding or the ability to capture its essence in articulated propositions.

Baseball tolerates doubt, even that which easily could be resolved. It embraces the poetry of human judgment rather than the science of instant replay. Except in a narrow area, home run calls where a boundary is in dispute, baseball forswears the clarity technology could provide; and this exception has only produced one memorable incident, when an Alex Rodriguez blast in the 2009 World Series hit a television camera in the field of play and was ruled a home run, though baseball officials are considering some expansion of the technology's use. This new approach, however, is not without at least some dissent in baseball's front office. In his post-managerial job working for the commissioner, Joe Torre put it this way: "The game isn't perfect. For all of us that want everything to be right all the time, that's not going to be the case, no matter how much replay you're going to see. I don't know why we want everything to be perfect. Life isn't perfect. I think this is a game of life, myself."

When umpire Jim Joyce blew a call at first base that cost Detroit Tiger pitcher Armando Galarraga what would have been the final out of a perfect game in 2010, thousands of fans and dozens of commentators and columnists petitioned baseball commissioner Bud Selig to invoke his "best interests of the game" power and overrule the call. Selig refused— even though by then Joyce had conceded his mistake.

During the 2012 baseball season, in a much less compelling case, the Mets actually offered their third baseman, David Wright, as sacrifice in an appeal to the league office of a ruling affecting what had gone in the books as a one-hitter by R. A. Dickey. Their appeal urged that the lone hit be turned into an error by Wright. Not surprisingly, especially given baseball's commitment to living in the gray zone of a human official scorer's judgment, the league office denied the request. Interestingly, Dickey threw another one-hitter in his very next start, becoming only the seventh person in modern baseball history to pitch back-to-back one-hitters. Ironically, earlier that same month, the first no-hitter in the Mets' fifty-year history had been thrown by Johan

Santana, saved only because the third base umpire ruled that a ball hit by St. Louis Cardinal Carlos Beltran landed foul—a ruling that would not have survived instant replay.

Don Denkinger called balls and strikes for thirty years but is best remembered for another incorrect call at first base that Cardinals fans will tell you cost their team the 1985 World Series against the Kansas City Royals. But umpires have always had the final word.

Baseball's seven-year experiment with QuesTec computer equipment to evaluate umpires' calls of balls and strikes is yet another example. According to the rule book, the strike zone stretches from the midpoint between the top of the batter's shoulders and the top of the uniform pants (usually around the letters of the uniform) to just below the knees. Horizontally, it's the width of home plate. But umpires have always added a dose of discretion. For years, the term *National League strike* referred to the more generous calls afforded to pitchers in the NL than the AL. Players knew how certain umps would call games, and they adjusted. It was "part of the game."

Once umpires' calls were placed under the microscope beginning in 2003, the strike zone started to change. And for finesse pitchers like Greg Maddux and Tom Glavine—both of whom built their Hall of Fame–bound careers by getting borderline strike calls, where their pitches may not have grazed the corner of the plate but came close enough—it shrunk. But the outcry that followed served as a reminder that the lords of baseball have always ruled that a strike isn't a strike because it fits neatly into a box; it's a strike simply because it is called one by an umpire. The very reason an umpire uses such bravado in making the call of "Strike!" on an obviously close pitch is to put a coating of certainty on what could be doubt. The game's rituals demand it; one of the quickest routes to an ejection from a game by an umpire is to argue a ball or strike call.

But baseball still has followers who would reduce the game to numbers and equations. And the intricate arithmetic of the game provides grist for the mills of such persons—the statisticians and trivia buffs who sometimes are celebrated and often regard themselves as the true aficionados.

The recent rise of sabermetrics—the analysis of baseball through complex statistical measures—has brought a new lexicon to the game, catapulted a new breed of general managers to prominence, and brought joy to those who delight in stats and trivia. Players are now scored on their OPS (an amalgam of on-base and slugging percentages) and BABIP (which measures how many balls in play against a pitcher go for hits), and there is much, much more. Stadium scoreboards and television broadcasts, supported by powerful search engines, announce how the batter at the plate has done in a certain inning, against a certain kind of pitcher, on a certain day of the week, in certain wind conditions; and this is supposed to help us enjoy the game. To some, such data is the key to understanding baseball; to others, myself included, it is reminiscent of medieval theologians debating the number of angels that could dance on the head of a pin.

Let me be clear. I love the intricate numbers of baseball. To this day, my son remembers how the two of us would work with a folded newspaper as I would teach him to decipher box scores. Yes, I taught him mathematics; but more important, I taught him baseball and I taught him love as we worked on those numbers together. It was a way for us to bond. There is wonder in the vast variety of numbers that baseball produces. And it is undeniable that sabermetrics provide valuable tools to the front office and fan alike; evidence of all kinds is critical to making good decisions—the more, the better.

But the most important elements of baseball cannot be measured. Some of them simply are immeasurable. And the numbers can miss the essence of the matter; the facts can become false idols, obscuring truth in horrible reductionism. Simply scribbling *F7* on a scorecard after a spectacular catch in left field doesn't capture the magic of the moment or the actual talent involved—just as musical notes on a sheet of paper cannot capture the beautiful sounds of a violin.

Sabermetrics will explain that most hitting and winning streaks stem not from determination or even luck but from a phenomenon known as a Poisson distribution, a mathematical expression in a gorgeously complicated equation of the probability of events occurring within a fixed period of time. The poet watching from the center field bleachers sees the game through a different lens entirely. The difference between sabermetrics and mystery is the difference between the veracity of Poisson distributions and the wonder of Joe DiMaggio's magical hitting streak.

Scientist and mystic "live at the portal between knowledge and mystery," wrote Chet Raymo. The scientist sees a piece of cloth that can be carbon dated or a glove whose provenance can be demonstrated. The mystic sees *through* the relic (The shroud in which Christ was wrapped? A glove Robinson wore?) to the mystery. But to subjugate one magisterium (in Stephen Jay Gould's words) to another, to see either science or religion as the only source of knowledge, is to narrow the search for truth, not to elevate it. Balance is the key; and doubt is a call to balance.

In Robert Coover's novel *The Universal Baseball Association, Inc., J. Henry Waugh, Prop.*, the eponymous Henry loses all sense of balance as he immerses himself in baseball's mountain of data. A melancholy accountant, he finds joy only from a game that he invented, a baseball league of pure fantasy played out on his kitchen table through dice and charts, where each roll helps determine the results of individual pitches, plays, games, and even entire seasons. Henry keeps records meticulously, calculating stats, which in turn provide the trends that shape subsequent "plays."

Ultimately, Henry (and the reader) is unsure which of his worlds is real. His simulated league is a destructive obsession. Henry's descent is gradual. Early on, he observes his league and its players from afar: "You roll, Player A gets a hit or he doesn't, gets his man out or he doesn't. Sounds simple. But call Player A 'Sycamore Flynn' or 'Melbourne Trench' and something starts to happen. He shrinks or grows, stretches out or puts on muscle." To Henry they become human, and he has feelings for them.

But later, after his favorite player is fatally struck by a line drive, a seemingly certain Henry intervenes in the world he has created, seeking not only retribution but also what he considers to be a restoration of balance (would God do this?). At the moment of Henry's intervention in *his* world, his relationship with the game and reality is transformed: "He picked up the dice, shook them. 'I'm sorry, boy,' he whispered, and then, holding the dice in his left palm, he set them down carefully with his right. One by one. Six. Six. Six. A sudden spasm convulsed him with the impact of a smashing line drive and he sprayed a red-and-golden rainbow arc of half-curded pizza over his Association, but he managed to get to the sink with most of it. And when he'd done his vomiting, when he'd finished, he went to bed and there slept a deep, deep sleep."

The Universal Baseball Association is a great story, deeply metaphysical and existential, and at its core a study in duality: free will and predestination, creationism and evolution, omnipotence and helplessness, certitude and doubt. It is commentary on Albert Einstein's famous dictum that God does not play dice with the universe. And it is no coincidence that J. Henry Waugh abbreviates to JHWH, a reference to the Old Testament Hebrew's spelling of Yahweh, the name of God. In becoming the Creator, Henry sacrifices his humanity, living in a world fixated on nothing but numbers.

Like Henry, many baseball fans are fascinated by the

facts and figures of the game. I am myself. But even for those
who do not become as obsessed as Henry Waugh, trivia can
easily become a Philistine's gambit, and here doubt serves us
well. Take the following tale as warning—or as a homily on
the importance of doubt even where faith abounds.

My friend Anthony Mannino (I call him Tippy) is a living encyclopedia of baseball. When I became dean of NYU's
School of Law in 1988, I started using a car service, and
Tippy, one of the drivers, became a fixture in my life and
those of my family and friends.

Tippy is a Damon Runyon character. A New Yorker to
his core, he is full of opinion, full of lore, and completely
without pretense. He can connect with anybody, often by
sharing his passion for baseball. And he is a veritable re-
pository of baseball "knowledge," although the following
will remind us that sometimes (maybe often) what we believe to be true is not and that many a sportswriter who
followed the Hall of Fame Yankee manager Casey Stengel's
challenge to "look it up" found a different story from the
one he told.

On rides to the ballpark, Tippy regales my guests with
fascinating accounts of the minutiae of the game. And over
the years, in an act of inexcusable intellectual theft, I have
often adopted Tippy's best questions and passed them off
as my own, usually to spark conversation during a dull game.
The two best, in my view, deal with New York players who
had accomplished rare feats—indeed, feats that (according
to Tippy) had been accomplished only once in the entire
history of the game.

Question one: Who is the only player in baseball history to have hit an inside-the-park grand slam home run?

As my interlocutor invariably struggled for the answer,
I would give a set of tantalizing clues. I would point out
that the batter was a pitcher (the outfielders were apt to be
playing shallow, making a ball hit over their heads more

likely); then I would remind my companion that in the old Yankee Stadium, the monuments in deep center field were in play, often causing outfielders to get confused when a ball caromed off them. To add a sense of relevance, if I were asking the question at a Yankees game, as was usually the case, I'd point out (until a few years ago) that "he's in the ballpark tonight," because the answer was the man who was for many years manager Joe Torre's pitching coach.

Mel Stottlemyre.

Question two: Who is the only player in baseball history to hit a home run in his first major league at-bat and a triple in his second?

My first hint would be that the player is in the Hall of Fame. Second—and this always raised some eyebrows—in a twenty-one-year career, the player never hit another home run or another triple. Third, among other feats he had pitched a no-hitter. And fourth, he was best known as a knuckleball-throwing relief pitcher. The last clue usually gave it away.

Hoyt Wilhelm.

I must have asked guests and friends these questions hundreds of times. At the first NYU commencement ceremony held in the new stadium, in May 2009, I challenged the graduates with the Stottlemyre question in my closing address. My offer to buy dinner for whoever contacted me with the correct answer went unclaimed.

Two months later, my friend Fred Wilpon called to invite me to a Mets game. Fred has made it a personal mission to try to convert me to the Mets (he's the majority owner), arguing that they're the natural descendants of the Dodgers.

Fred told me that he had invited another rabid Yankees fan who, as he put it, "should be a Mets fan as well," and said that I'd be surprised by how much the other guest knew about baseball. That person, it turned out, was Henry Kissinger. I brought with me my colleague Katy Fleming, who runs NYU's campuses in Europe, and whom Fred had invited when I told him she was in town.

What Fred and I had forgotten was that Katy, like Kissinger, is an expert in European history. As the game progressed, the two delved into a heated discussion on the Congress of Vienna, Klemens von Metternich, and how the world might be if events had unfolded differently in the nineteenth century (the words *infield fly rule* were never uttered). Fred and I rolled our eyes: The two had lost their sense of place and time. Worse yet, the game was too listless to draw them back to us.

To fill the void, I launched into my standard ball game discourse. "Dr. Kissinger, if I can interrupt. I know you are having a great conversation with Katy about history, but I'm going to restore your faith in the research university by dazzling you with some baseball history that—even as omniscient as you are—you do not know."

"I don't think you can stump me," said Kissinger in his uniquely deep and gravelly voice. "Let's see you try."

I launched into the Stottlemyre question. Kissinger and Wilpon wrestled with it until I finally revealed the answer. In an instant, Kissinger reminded me that in the wake of the 9/11 attacks, he had filmed a commercial to boost New York City tourism that featured his lifelong dream coming true. ("Everybody has a New York dream, come find yours" was the tag line.) His dream: hitting an inside-the-park home run at Yankee Stadium. "They actually made me hit the ball, but thank God they didn't have me run the bases," he said. Instead they used a double.

Then I dazzled them with the Wilhelm question. Kissinger conceded: "I would not have believed that, in all the games that have been played, there would be things that have happened only once."

Meanwhile, the game started to get more interesting. Down 3–1 to the Colorado Rockies in the bottom of the sixth, the Mets rallied and scored two runs. The score remained 3–3 until the bottom of the eighth, when Fernando Tatis, in the twilight of a journeyman career, hit what turned out to be a game-winning grand slam home run for New York. The Mets won 7–3.

As we headed down in the elevator with a group of jubilant fans, I decided to give Tippy, who was picking me up after the game, a quick call to tell him I was coming. Reliable as always, he produced another interesting "fact," which I shared with Kissinger, Fred, and the captive audience of twenty or so people who were jammed in the elevator with us.

"Ladies and gentlemen," I intoned, "did you know that there is only one player in the history of baseball who has hit two grand slam home runs in the same inning?" Silence. Not a guess. A chorus, led by Kissinger, of "Who was it?"

"That person," I said, "was Fernando Tatis, the man we saw hit the game-winning grand slam tonight." They were genuflecting as I walked toward the car, where Tippy, the man behind the curtain to whom I never gave credit for the trivia, waited eagerly to discuss the game.

It took another two weeks before my certitude was shaken. This time I was at a game in Yankee Stadium with my friend Jay Furman and his son, Jesse. The game was slow, so out came the Stottlemyre question.

Jesse, a pugnacious Yale Law School graduate who since has become a federal judge after a career as a prosecutor, challenged me right away. "That can't be true," he said. I assured him that it was, invoked my stature as a university president and a scholar-fan, and quietly bristled at his doubt.

Within an inning, Jesse, using his BlackBerry, had discovered a list of forty players, Stottlemyre barely noticeable among them, who had hit an inside-the-park grand slam since 1950. Eight had done it since 1990. Roberto Clemente once ended a game that way, and Brooklyn's Jimmy Sheckard did it in consecutive games in 1901. In the face of this overwhelming evidence, my first response (echoing many religious leaders past) was to deny the evidence and to affirm what I believed: "The Internet is full of misinformation," I said—unconvincingly, even to me.

After the game, I confronted Tippy. He reacted as have true believers through the centuries. "If that bastard Jesse Furman hadn't looked that up, you and I would have gone to our graves thinking that Stottlemyre was the only one to do it. And we'd be a lot better off." Then he added, "The amazing thing is you've told hundreds of people, and I've told hundreds of people, and nobody has ever denied it." Everyone had accepted what they were told as fact even though, by the law of averages, at least a few of the folks we told likely would have seen one of the home runs hit since 1990 on TV or even in person.

Tippy may still have been certain, but I was not. Like many over the centuries whose faith has been challenged by doubt, I started to consider the logical extension of what had just happened and asked, "If what you told me about Stottlemyre wasn't true, how could I believe what you told me about Wilhelm?" I had begun to doubt. Tippy responded with a reaffirmation of infallibility worthy of a pope or a shaman who had forecast rain on a dry day or an apocalyptic leader who foresaw the end of the world on a date now passed: "You can take everything else that I've told you to the bank; I guarantee it."

And so I rested . . . until my son called shortly thereafter to report more trouble (or should I say new knowledge): Wilhelm had hit a home run in his first at-bat; in his second time up, he grounded out to the pitcher. He had five other hits (all singles) during his first year in the majors. The triple didn't come for another year. And, yes, he never hit another home run or triple after those first ones.

So Tippy's "dogma" could be restated (in full conformity with the newly discovered facts) as follows: There is only one person in the history of baseball who hit a homer in his first at-bat and a triple the following year, and who over a career of at least ten years (Wilhelm played for twenty) never hit a home run or triple again. The Hall of Fame and the magnificent knuckleball could still be tantalizing clues.

I suggested this to Tippy; but as before, he was uninterested in the revised story, faithful as it was to the facts.

Tippy faced his moral crisis of faith and made his choice, but I had a choice to make as well. Over the years, violating all academic rules of attribution, I had presented myself (not Tippy) to my companions (now including Henry Kissinger) as the knowing source. I had accepted their plaudits like a keeper of Gnostic truths. Should I now reveal to those I had misinformed over the years that neither Stottlemyre nor Wilhelm stood alone in history, as I had claimed? In particular, should I tell Kissinger, who (I was pretty certain) was likely appropriating the information as his own, thereby putting a reputation far more important than mine at stake?

As I said to Tippy, "It's one thing if my reputation is ruined. With Henry Kissinger, world peace is at stake!" To this day, I have not told Secretary Kissinger.

Tippy's tale reveals the perils of hubris and certitude, unleavened by doubt. And it displays the ways those who claim the Truth with a capital *T*—religious or otherwise, from popes to drivers—react when science (the advancement of what we know) throws into question the basis of belief. Tippy simply would not let the facts get in the way.

Of course, though facts may not capture the ineffable truths, they do yield truth. And it is up to people of faith to resolve conflicts between religion and science. As Chet Raymo put it: "Science cannot resolve the conflict between science and faith; science must go wherever it is led by the empirical method, peeling away the veils in which nature hides. If the conflict between science and religion is to be resolved, it is up to persons of faith to modify their (tenets), and indeed this has been happening since the beginning of human history. Most Catholics, for example, no longer talk about banishing unbaptized babies to Limbo or believe Genesis offers a literal account of creation. The Index of Forbidden Books is gone, Galileo has been rehabilitated. . . . And when all the magical thinking is gone, what are we left with? With plenty. Faith communities *at their best* add immeasurably to the storehouse of human well-being."

So it is that even for those who delight in the great gifts of science, faith sometimes arises to conquer doubt. When it comes varies and often is unknown. After the Minnesota Twins won the 1991 World Series (the only one in history played between the two teams that had finished last the year before), in extra innings, pitcher Jack Morris revealed how, before Game Seven, "a total peace" had washed over him—instilling a complete confidence that with the ball in his hand, the Twins would be world champions. "I knew I could not lose," Morris remembers. He pitched a ten-inning shutout and the Twins won, 1–0.

That same inner confidence had sustained another brash pitcher, Johnny Podres of the Brooklyn Dodgers, as he prepared to face the favored Yankees in Game Seven of the Series in 1955. Barely twenty-three, Podres knew about the Dodgers' long string of agonizing disappointments, but he did not feel their oppressive weight. Simple faith swallowed the doubts of history. On the team bus ride to Yankee Stadium, a tightly wound Podres paced the aisle, exhorting his teammates to just score one run, saying that was all he needed. As it turned out, they scored twice; but like Morris, Podres only needed one to win the game that gave Brooklyn its only World Series.

With doubt and faith inextricably intertwined, how does *belief* arise? For many believers, as my journalist pals say of some tales, they are too good to check out. But that belittles faith.

It sometimes may be acceptable to sustain doubt even where it could be resolved. Such is the case for me with my "original 1955 Jackie Robinson glove," or for baseball with its umpires largely unsupported by instant replay. These are style choices, not faith.

On other occasions, the seeds of doubt are dubiously sown—and we must be doubtful about the doubt itself. This is especially the case in the age of the Internet, when anyone can say anything and anything can achieve wide distribution, and the defamation has become as simple as a click of the "send" button on a computer screen. Doubt is then created, even if virtually out of thin air.

Consider a case involving Gil Hodges, the first baseman of the Brooklyn Dodgers, beloved to this day forty years following his death way too young at forty-seven, who was the manager of the Miracle Mets team that won the World Series in 1969. In the climactic fifth game, an incident occurred that still stirs arguments. With the Mets trailing 3–0, the Baltimore Oriole pitcher, Dave McNally, threw a very low pitch to the Mets hitter, Cleon Jones. When the ball landed, it then made a sharp turn and bounced all the way into the Mets' dugout. The only question was whether it hit Jones's foot (the rules say you are awarded first base whether you are hit on the bounce or on the fly); despite Jones's protestations, home plate umpire Lou DiMuro called the pitch a ball.

Within seconds, however, Hodges appeared at home plate to show DiMuro a baseball, and spotting a black mark indicating shoe polish, the umpire overruled himself and awarded Jones first base. (Knowledgeable fans quickly remembered a similar incident that turned around a pivotal game in the 1957 World Series involving Yankee pitcher Tommy Byrne and a Milwaukee Braves pinch hitter, Nippy Jones.) The next batter, Donn Clendenon, hit a home run off the possibly unsettled McNally, igniting a Mets comeback that won the game and thus the Series a few innings later.

Forty years passed, until at a Mets reunion their pitching star that day, Jerry Koosman, told reporters a fresh tale: When the ball bounced into the Mets' dugout right to him, Hodges quickly told him to rub it on his shoe and hand it back, an underhanded maneuver if ever there was one. If true, the tale would tarnish Hodges's impeccable reputation, hard won over the years. Koosman's claim, however, never got much traction until it was revived and passed on uncritically in a new Hodges biography published in 2012 and then repeated in book reviews.

But there's a reason it had never received much traction to begin with: There was absolutely no evidence to support it. For one thing, no less than Hall of Fame pitcher Tom Seaver, also in the dugout that day, reminded inquiring reporters that Koosman (a well-spoken farm boy from rural Minnesota) had a deserved reputation as both a practical joker and a teller of tall tales. For still another, the batter, Cleon Jones, angrily protested that it was inconceivable Hodges could have thought of such a trick and had it executed in a split second.

Further muddying the waters, retired Mets outfielder Ron Swoboda has still another recollection of the incident. According to Swoboda, the ball in question had actually bounced onto a bag of baseballs stored in the dugout, and in his haste to get to home plate Hodges had by chance picked up a ball with a mark on it.

That's four different stories from four people who were there that day. If nothing else, this story is a useful reminder about the lives of the saints; no saint would claim perfection and no saint would have others claim it on his behalf. Hodges, a devout Catholic, would surely agree.

However, it is not acceptable as a general matter to resist the investigations and discovery that translates what today is unknown into what tomorrow (or a hundred years from now) will be known. And this is not the role of faith, for genuine faith is not calculated to avoid inconvenient truths or prolong ignorance.

The moral of these tales is that doubt matters and often matters greatly. One of its synonyms is *skepticism*, a word often linked in its positive connotations with the adjective *healthy* in the most demanding intellectual circles. Through the centuries, the power of doubt and healthy skepticism has often been trained on world religions and their faithful. And given the horrors wreaked by the armies who carried Truth into battle or invoked it in the persecution of others, such criticism is justified. In the secular domain, moreover, doubt is part of the foundation of the scientific method in particular and of most serious inquiry in general. It is doubt that drives the expansion of the reality of what we know and the reduction of the realm of the unknown. The warning that certitude sounds, whether in religion or in science, should trigger it.

On the other hand, doubt needs a rational foundation, a solid logical or factual basis. It should not be idle or mischievous, the simplistic act of casting aspersions—like the mere tossing of a pebble into still water to observe the rippling result. It is no accident that in the legal community the adjective most often associated with doubt is the properly demanding word *reasonable*.

Then there is the ineffable, the unknowable, where doubt also resides. Here, only faith can fill the emptiness.

In the end, there *is*, however, one absolute truth, one certitude that admits no doubt: Fernando Tatis is the only player in the history of baseball to hit two grand slams in the same inning. You can take it to the bank; I guarantee it. Don't even bother to look it up.

Well, maybe you should.

A dozen years before my son was born, the Dodgers left Brooklyn for California, breaking my heart but not my spirit.

The betrayal of millions of devoted fans, especially the young ones like me who were experiencing adult misbehavior for the first time, produced myriad reactions. In my case, the last thing I would have expected in those dark days of 1958 was that I would end up rooting for the hated New York Yankees; but that is what happened.

Just not at first. During the Dodgers' early years in Los Angeles, some of their old Brooklyn fans gave up on baseball; some moved their allegiance (if not their love) to other teams; and some, like me, continued to follow the Dodgers from afar. I was as passionate about them as ever, tracking wins and losses painstakingly and calculating the statistics of my favorite players via the box scores printed in the late edition of the New York *Daily Mirror*. I was resolved not to abandon something that had been at the core of my identity since the first moment I experienced the green glory of Ebbets Field, watched Jackie Robinson patrolling the infield, and heard the mellifluous radio tones of first Red Barber and then Vin Scully.

As I came of age, the Dodgers rewarded my continent-spanning devotion in at least one area where they had disappointed in Brooklyn—they won consistently. Indeed, in their first eight years after being kidnapped from Brooklyn, the Dodgers won the World Series three times. And often I could catch their games on TV, in part because of the national fascination with their stunning pitching staff—anchored by Don Drysdale, Claude Osteen, and Brooklyn's own Sandy Koufax, the greatest of them all. In 1966, when they won yet another National League pennant, I joined a group of the Dodger diaspora in Baltimore to see the final two games of the World Series. They lost a pair of 1–0 contests, ending the Series on the wrong side of four maddening games. All the while it never occurred to me that I would soon be embracing another team. My faith remained strong.

Jed changed everything. In addition to a name, a home, a family, and my love, I was determined to give my son a baseball team to enjoy. With the Dodgers a continent away, and the Mets too recently arrived, the Yankees and their great tradition beckoned. I could envision reliving the delight of a son and a father together at a ball game rooting for the same team, this time with me in the role of father.

Initially, I continued to root for the Dodgers—quietly. Sure, I'd root for the Yankees when I would take Jed to the Stadium, teaching him about their past and present and about the splendor of the game along the way; but I just couldn't shake my memories of all the heart-wrenching defeats they handed to the Dodgers, 1955 notwithstanding. Given the firewall that separated the American and National Leagues at the time (it was still decades before the start of interleague play), I was never forced to make a true choice, and as a result, Jed was shielded from knowing anything of my dueling allegiances.

The turning point came in 1977. The Yankees, having shaken off the cobwebs of a woeful decade, made it to their second straight World Series under new owner George Steinbrenner, who used the newly created tool of free agency to buy future Hall of Fame players Catfish Hunter and Reggie Jackson. In the 1977 World Series, the Yankees faced the Dodgers, who had stunned the powerhouse Cincinnati Reds in a divisional race and then beat a favored Philadelphia Phillies team to win the pennant.

Jed was eight years old and a fully engaged fan. Remaining even a closet Dodgers fan would have pitted me against his hopes; that was unthinkable. And so it was that the first pitch of Game One from ex-Red-now-Yankee Don Gullett to Davey Lopes of the Dodgers amounted to something much more significant to me than the start of a series or even a World Series; it was my moment of conversion.

When the same teams met again the following autumn, no personal conflict or dilemma or feeling of nostalgia urged me back toward the Dodgers. I had my new faith, and it remains with me today.

My colleague Eric Klinenberg, a prolific author (most recently of the bestselling study of America's social patterns, *Going Solo*), had a similar journey. As he put it in *New York* magazine in 2009:

> I grew up on the North Side of Chicago during the seventies and eighties and was raised to love the woeful Cubs. Spare me your pity. Sure, my team never came close to a pennant. . . . Sure, every year I dreamed of a championship, and every year those dreams were dashed. But my team had perfected the art of failure, and I never expected anything more.

Now I live in New York City, and I have a three-year-old son. Of course, I wanted him to fall for Chicago's lovable losers. [However] a hometown team would be better, I knew. But I grew up in the shadow of the Miracle Mets of 1969, and I still resent them. The Yankees? God forbid. With twenty-six titles and the culture of entitlement that comes with them, the franchise offends those of us raised in Wrigleyville. So really, what choice did I have?

Also, I admit, I believed that my son might be the one we'd been waiting for, the guy who would turn the Cubs' luck around. And then something incredible happened. In 2007, his first full season, the Cubs made the playoffs. My grandmother bought him a cap and T-shirt. I persuaded my wife to let him stay up late to watch the games on TV. I'll confess that it hurt when the Diamondbacks swept us 3–0 in the first round. But we were off to a promising start.

The next year was better. The Cubs were sensational all season. They cruised into the playoffs with the best record in the National League and had home-field advantage against the Dodgers. Once again, I outfitted my boy in Cubs regalia and got him permission to stay up late to watch the games. I taught him to say Soriano, Lee, and, yes, Fukudome, to sing "root, root, root for the Cubbies" during the seventh-inning stretch.

But it didn't matter. The Cubs lost the first game of the NLDS badly, the second game worse. Then they went to Los Angeles and were swept again. I couldn't help asking: What was I doing to my child?

This year I vowed to do things differently. No, I didn't renounce the Cubs. But I didn't replace his Cubs cap when he lost it, either. In June I did the unthinkable: I bought him a Yankees hat, classic black, then another, in red. I got us tickets to see the Red Sox at the new ballpark. Gave him a baseball signed by all the Yankees and a plastic batting helmet filled with ice cream. We started reading the sports page together, cheering each time the Yankees triumphed. "I love the Yankees because they're winners," he announced one day. And though I smiled, I also felt my heart sink.

Last week, the Yankees won their twenty-seventh World Series. Yes, those of us from Chicago are counting, too. My son was jubilant. He learned to say Matsui, made the Yankees symbol with Play-Doh, and asked if we could go to the parade.

Part of me wonders if I did the right thing. My son is now a Yankees fan, as is his birthright, and so he carries a burden. He may never be content in a second city. He may expect, even demand, a championship each year. He may not develop the character that comes from enduring disappointment, nor have faith that fidelity and suffering will be rewarded someday.

Then again, he has already experienced a World Series title, something neither my grandmother (now ninety-one) nor I have done. I suppose I'm a bit envious, but mostly I'm enjoying his—okay, *our*, November happiness.

Maybe next year I'll get my own Yankees cap. Then again, next year may belong to the Cubs.

My journey from the Dodgers to the Yankees (like Eric's from the Cubs to the Yanks) did not take me back to the pain and thrills of my youth; it took me forward to something else. Any comparison is apples and oranges, absurd on its face. For me, the affection is no less strong or meaningful;

for me the New York Yankees of today are not—in an existential sense—the Yankees who vexed the post–World War II Brooklyn Dodgers. Such has been my journey.

And I am not alone. The renowned British writer C. S. Lewis once asked rhetorically, "Is God a clown who whips away your bowl of soup one moment in order, next moment, to replace it with another bowl of the same soup? Even nature isn't such a clown as that. She never plays exactly the same tune twice."

Conversion is not for the faint of heart. It can begin with a dramatic external event; or it can be the result of a lengthy period of reexamination and introspection. It is a difficult process, requiring effort and perseverance. In baseball, at least sometimes, it can be entirely about the future, requiring no rejection of previous allegiance; nothing can ever disturb the special place the Brooklyn Dodgers occupy in my heart. But a spiritual conversion looks both forward and backward. Our previous allegiances are, in the end, rejected, even as our new one is faithfully embraced. All the great stories—the modern ones like C. S. Lewis's diligent journey and the ones from antiquity like Paul and Augustine—leave something behind as the great leap forward is taken.

What the two worlds share is an infinite variety of journeys down a multitude of paths. I was hardly alone, for example, in having to process the loss of my Brooklyn Dodgers. By no means have all who processed it experienced what I did or even experienced a conversion. But many have.

Each spring, for my final class at NYU, I have two writers, good friends each, visit to talk about the Dodgers as wonderful leitmotifs and metaphors for their youth. Their stories of conversion are quite different from mine.

The eminent historian Doris Kearns Goodwin is today one of the best-known, most delightfully fervent citizens of

Red Sox Nation. As in my case, Doris's was not a sudden or easy transformation from her deep Dodger roots growing up in Rockville Centre on Long Island. But as she explains in her bestselling memoir *Wait Till Next Year* (the famous, defiant, unfortunately annual cry of Dodgers fans everywhere), her transformation was complete within twenty years of the departure that broke her heart.

My collaborator on this book Tom Oliphant, the author of the bestseller *Praying for Gil Hodges*, after a lifetime in political journalism, has gradually realized that the team passion of his youth cannot be replicated for him. His passion today is for the game itself and is every bit as intense as he once felt about one team, though he confesses happiness still at the passage of any October without another World Series championship for the Yankees.

Together, our trinity of stories represents the angst and anguish over the Dodgers' move felt in every corner of Brooklyn and the vast Brooklyn diaspora. They are a sampling of just some of the divergent paths that frustrated fans were compelled to travel.

It is interesting to note the ways in which we went about our journeys and how each journey mirrors the nature of religious conversion. Each of us gravitated toward one of what Paul Tillich described as building blocks of faith: actual experience, my methodical search for a team after the birth of my son; surrender, Doris's baseball transformation based entirely on feeling and emotion; or acceptance, Tom's measured reconnection with the game he loves.

Each of us was an adolescent when the possibility that the Dodgers might leave slowly morphed into probability. Each of us had the most intimate ties imaginable to our Dodgers, through our fathers at first and then through our own experiences. But each of us could see and interpret the depressingly numerous signs that something terrible was going to happen. It might have been the heinous attempted trade of Jackie Robinson to the detested Harlem rival New York Giants (thank God Jackie retired instead after the 1956 season); it might have been a strange schedule that included "home" games across the Hudson River in Jersey City; it might have been the first appearance in the newspapers of those two dreaded words, *Los Angeles* (anything but the "City of Angels" to us).

As Doris put it, "In 1957, the auguries of Brooklyn's betrayal began to multiply. . . . Every day a new piece was added to the dismal puzzle."

She signed one of the many fan petitions that were circulated that spring and summer; she attended a "Keep the Dodgers" rally in the city; she wrote an impassioned letter to the Dodgers' infamous boss, Walter O'Malley; she even daydreamed about going to see him in her favorite dress and high heels, successfully persuading him not to do the unthinkable that would eventually become the unforgivable.

To no avail. Poignantly, she follows an account of the crushing announcement and the Dodgers' last game at storied Ebbets Field with an account of the final decline of her mother's health (she had battled serious problems for years), which began that same awful September.

Doris did not merely wander in the baseball wilderness after her beloved team abandoned her; she rejected the wilderness entirely.

In her words, "Although time and events outdistanced and reconciled my personal losses, my anger over O'Malley's treason still persisted. At Colby College and in my first year at Harvard—where I would teach for almost a decade before leaving to become a full-time historian—I refused to follow baseball, skipping over the sports pages with their accounts of alien teams called the Los Angeles Dodgers and the San Francisco Giants."

It was a date during the second year of her doctoral work

that changed everything; it brought her from Cambridge on the subway to Fenway Park, more than intimate enough and filled with more than enough people who knew their baseball to awaken a dormant fan's deep needs and memories. And her timing was impeccable, her reawakening coming just as the Red Sox were beginning to emerge from a period of almost boring incompetence to truly torment their fans with famously close calls—another link to her past.

"For years," as she put it, "I had managed to stay away. I had formed the firmest of resolutions. I had given myself irrefutable reasons, expressed the most passionate of rejections. But I could not get away. Addiction or obsession, love or need, I was born a baseball fan and a baseball fan I was fated to remain."

In a few years, talking baseball again with her father during pennant races (his fatal heart attack came in 1972 while he was watching his adopted Mets play on television)—she had converted. In 2007, as the Red Sox fought toward their second championship since 1918, she announced her candidacy for president of Red Sox Nation, a fan organization. Her principal opponents were Jerry Remy (a former second baseman and popular broadcaster) and a local teacher and coach who called himself Regular Rob Crawford.

At the candidates' night in a tavern near Fenway Park, however, she found herself nodding in agreement as Crawford argued a simple proposition passionately: A regular fan was in a better position to do more for other ordinary fans. She promptly withdrew from the race in his favor.

"Sometimes, sitting in the park with my boys," she wrote in her memoir, "I imagine myself back at Ebbets Field, a young girl once more in the presence of my father, watching the players of my youth on the grassy fields below—Jackie Robinson, Duke Snider, Roy Campanella, Gil Hodges. There is magic in these moments, for when I open my eyes and see my sons in the place where my father once sat, I feel an invisible bond among our three generations, an anchor of loyalty and love linking my sons to the grandfather whose face they have never seen but whose person they have come to know through this most timeless of sports."

It is this experience, an opening of oneself to an ineffable connection to something greater, that Tillich characterized as *surrendering* to faith. He described the transformation as an "awakening from a state in which an ultimate concern is lacking (or more exactly, hidden) to an open and conscious awareness of it. If conversion means this, every spiritual experience is an experience of conversion."

Doris's experience at the ballpark, sitting next to her sons while reflecting on her father, transported her to another plane. It conjured feelings that allowed for a break from ordinary time and place, enabling her to touch the transcendent, where the sacred manifests itself through what many would consider the profane. To the uninitiated, that vehicle appears to be a mere game; but for Doris, and countless fans like her, baseball possessed a powerful capacity to induce this sensation and stir the feelings of childhood: excitement and anticipation, sorrow and joy. The Red Sox of today took her back to the Dodgers of yesterday, when she lived the game alongside her dad. In this sense, the process of conversion has actually brought Doris *closer* to her original baseball faith than would have otherwise been possible.

Tom's tale is different. As he tells it:

During the first year the Dodgers were gone my father insisted I look up and learn the meaning of the word *void*. Something that had filled so much of my young life, with my family and on my own, was simply gone, disappeared. And absolutely nothing existed or even loomed indistinctly on my horizon to take its place, leading me to suspect that nothing could. The initial blow was nothing compared to the daily reminders of the void as time passed.

I remember early in that first season, 1958, when the Dodgers came east to play the Phillies, my father declared we were going to go cross-town to Pennsylvania Station, hop a train for Philadelphia and see them—perhaps rekindle a little of the old feelings or at least assuage the pain for an afternoon (it was a Saturday).

Nothing of the sort happened. The Phillies by then were playing alone in ancient Connie Mack Stadium, the Athletics (whose Hall of Fame manager and executive gave the ballpark its name) having departed for Kansas City four years earlier, ironically the year after the name change from the original Shibe Park. It was even older than Ebbets Field and therefore offered an intimacy and feel that was at least generally familiar to me. We sat in upper deck grandstand seats on the third base side.

My parents and I made no noise whatsoever, not when the Dodgers' lineup was introduced, not when they took the field. For all the supposed kick of seeing Snider, Hodges, Reese, and Carl Furillo again, I still remember how weird they looked in the familiar blue caps with LA instead of B stitched on them. I also remember being attracted by the skills of a few of the Phillies' better players (Richie Ashburn in center field, Robin Roberts pitching) that I used to pray would fail or get hurt. We resolved, solemnly, never to go there again. And then the strangest thing happened.

We moved to California in the middle of the 1959 season.

My father, mostly disabled from his service in the Pacific during World War II, desperately needed the change and so we went, and landed just south of Los Angeles in the middle of a pennant race. Apart from the violent cultural change (I'm pretty sure I had never seen truly blond hair that didn't come out of a bottle), I had to confront the Dodgers in our near-backyard. My parents and I did it by rooting for them, not cheering for them. The personification of this new, odd stance for us was a new Dodger arrival that year named Wally Moon—a mean-looking man from Arkansas who appeared to rarely shave, but who for a few years appeared designed genetically for the weird confines of the majestic Los Angeles Coliseum—the team's temporary home while its new stadium was being constructed on the other side of the city. Fitting a baseball field inside of it required a very short left field foul line, only 250 feet, backed up by a 40-foot screen to keep at least some routine fly balls from being home runs. In 1959 especially, Moon specialized in sending several towering flies just over the barrier. Moon Shots, they were called, and they were my first thought when Bucky Dent's fluke fly landed in the netting behind the wall at Fenway Park nearly twenty years later. They all counted, but they never felt or looked genuine.

As I came of age, I continued to root instead of cheer. All through high school, Vin Scully was an almost nightly guest in our house on the radio. I was in college when the Dodgers swept the Yankees in 1963 and trounced the Twins (née the Washington Senators) two years later in the first World Series between two transplanted teams. It was in 1967, at the dawn of my writing life, that I first realized how much I had changed. I had gotten caught up in the fascination with the Red Sox's improbable Impossible Dream season that culminated in a pennant on the final day of the season. Enduring the first of three seven-game World Series defeats for the exasperating team, I was struck by how fascinated I had become watching the St. Louis Cardinals' ace Bob Gibson pitch, as he won three games in the Series, including the deciding seventh. I had gradually become devoted as much to the game as to any town or any team. I simply loved the experience of being in a ballpark and absorbing a game. But unlike John Sexton and very much like Doris Kearns Goodwin, what has survived from my time with the Brooklyn Dodgers is my total inability to wish the Yankees anything but ill.

For most of my life, I had difficulty describing, much less analyzing my intense devotion to the game, but it all became clear when I started hanging out at Sexton's NYU class. The reading that woke me up was the John Updike poem "Tao in the Yankee Stadium Bleachers." Almost at once it was clear to me, as to Updike, that "distance brings proportion." From that distance, where the stadium and the players and the fans are as one vast tableau, the unity of the scene is awesome and elevating. For me, the best moment is when a batter gets an extra-base hit with men already aboard and everyone on the field moves in gorgeous patterns that would move George Balanchine.

I imagine Professor Eliade agreeing that the effect can be ineffable. And as hierophanies go, it certainly works for me, with my journey from Dodger nut to baseball nut complete.

Each of the three of us spent some time wandering, even floundering, after the Dodgers abandoned us. Each of us stopped at more than one baseball way station on our different paths to figuring it all out. And each of us recognized that we were not trifling with trivial issues. We converted eventually to something quite different from our baseball origins, and each of us took quite a while and more than one twist and turn. No blinding revelations for any of us on our separate roads to Damascus.

Our stories stand in sharp contrast with the Christian story of conversion on that road, the story of Saint Paul. Saul of Tarsus—tent maker, tormentor of Christians, possibly a complicit witness to the killing of Saint Stephen—was traveling to Damascus to round up Christians when he was literally blinded by a bright light and, by his account, heard the voice of the resurrected Jesus Christ. The voice commanded him to fast and wait in Damascus, where his blindness was ended, and his instructions to spread the Word issued by another man, Ananias, who also got his instructions directly.

This story of Paul, arguably the second most important voice in the New Testament, is a story of revelation, not process. (As an aside, one of my political heroes, Adlai Stevenson—when asked what he thought of the statement by a prominent conservative Christian of his day, Norman Vincent Peale, that God would look favorably on Dwight D. Eisenhower's election as president—famously said that in matters of theology he found Paul appealing and Peale appalling.)

Paul's conversion occurs at Christianity's dawn. Down through the centuries a multitude of conversions have occurred not in revelatory blasts of light but through difficult, lengthy processes involving diligent introspection—none better than a spiritual journey that began in North Africa centuries later.

In the fourth century, Augustine had a father who was pagan and worldly, and a mother (eventually Saint Monica) who spent more than thirty years trying to convert her son to Christianity. He resisted mightily, obtaining an excellent education, worldly success, and apparently a deserved reputation for what might charitably be called hedonism (among other evidence, there was a child out of wedlock). Eventually settled in Milan, he was influenced by another early Christian, Saint Ambrose, and by the writings of Paul. Persuaded in his head, he resisted changing his wild ways, agreeing with the faith's tenets but still hooked on hedonism and famously pleading "not yet" to avoid changing. Finally converted, he spent the next forty years in the church hierarchy helping shape it and producing a mountain of prose that lasts to this day and rivals Paul's in its advocacy of a simple, reverent life.

In the twentieth century, C. S. Lewis took a similar journey, as much of the head as of the heart and soul. A product of a comfortable, conventionally Anglican family in Belfast, Clive Staples Lewis at first rejected the religion of his childhood, moving as a well-educated, witty young man into a lifelong interest in folktales and fantasy fiction; for many years he was what we could call a practicing atheist. Quite vocal in his aggressive nonbelief, he observed once that he was "very angry at God for not existing."

Lewis's conversion, commencing around the age of thirty, came in two stages—to belief in a higher power and then to Christianity. The process, described extensively in Lewis's books, was intriguingly self-analytical, bordering on the logical and surely not merely emotional. It was a continuous struggle, resulting (he once wrote) in the "most dejected and reluctant convert in all England."

This great man's spiritualism came in part from his growing appreciation of the transcendent forces around him in nature, in painting, sculpture, and music, and in encounters with others both directly and through reading. In particular, for an appreciation of a larger force at work, he leaned on the concept of the "numinous" (a supernatural presence) in the writings of Rudolf Otto, he of *mysterium tremendum et fascinans*. Through a reading of Otto and his own introspection, Lewis came to believe in God—the numinous, ineffable God described by Abraham Joshua Heschel: "The sense of the ineffable is a sense for transcendence, a sense for the allusiveness of reality to a super-rational meaning. The ineffable, then, is a synonym for hidden meaning rather than for absence of meaning. It stands for a dimension, which in the Bible is called glory, a dimension so real and sublime that it stuns our ability to adore it and fills us with awe rather than curiosity." As Lewis, looking back, put it: "Atheism turns out to be too simple. If the whole universe has no meaning, we should never have found out that it has no meaning."

The next step in Lewis's conversion also was partly derivative. None of his relationships was closer or more intense than his long friendship with the fervently Catholic writer and fellow Oxford man J. R. R. Tolkien, who shared his devotion to folktales (how fitting that the two of them produced two of the most compelling and bestselling works of fantasy fiction ever in *The Chronicles of Narnia* and *The Lord of the Rings*). In the end, prompted by a long conversation after dinner one evening in 1931, Lewis became a Christian, remaining one until his death in 1963. As he wrote:

> There was a man born among these Jews who claimed to be, or to be the son of, or to be "one with," the Something which is at once the awful haunter of nature and the giver of the moral law. The claim is so shocking—a paradox, and even a horror, which we may be easily lulled into taking too lightly—that only two views of this man are possible. Either he

was a raving lunatic of an unusually abominable type, or else He was, and is, precisely what He said. There is no middle way.

If the records make the first hypothesis unacceptable, you must submit to the second. And if you do that, all else that is claimed by Christians becomes credible—that this Man, having been killed, was yet alive, and that His death, in some manner incomprehensible to human thought, has effected a real change in our relations to the "awful" and "righteous" Lord, and a change in our favour.

Suffusing Lewis's work, in addition to the surpassing clarity of his self-analysis and deductive powers, is an eloquent sense of his struggles—toward faith and with it. "I didn't go to religion to make me happy," he wrote. "I always knew a bottle of Port would do that. If you want a religion to make you feel really comfortable, I certainly don't recommend Christianity." Fans of the Brooklyn Dodgers and Boston Red Sox would murmur amen.

Tillich, another contemporary of Lewis, described the purpose of his own writing as "to convince some readers of the hidden power of faith within themselves and of the infinite significance of that to which faith is related." Faith to Tillich is "the state of being ultimately concerned," believing in "the promise of ultimate fulfillment," and submitting to "the demand of total surrender to the subject of ultimate concern."

The word *concern* describes the affective or motivational aspect of human experience; the word *ultimate* signifies that the concern must be of an unconditional, absolute, or unqualified character. The meaning of the term *ultimate* is to be found in a particular person's experience rather than in some external reality. Tillich's argument, therefore, is that the concerns of any individual can be ranked, and that if we probe deeply enough, we will discover the underlying concern that gives meaning and orientation to a person's whole life. It is of this kind of experience, Tillich taught, that religions are made—and as a consequence, every person is endowed at his or her core with religion; what remains is the journey to discovery.

In Tillich's well-known portrait *Dynamics of Faith,* he described how within a human being the rational and the nonrational coexist: "Man is able to decide for or against reason, he is able to create beyond reason or to destroy below reason. . . . Faith is not an act of any of his rational functions, as it is not an act of the unconscious, but it is an act [*via conversion*] in which both the rational and the nonrational elements of his being are transcended."

Or as he wrote elsewhere, "Conversion is not a matter of prevailing arguments, but it is a matter of personal surrender," a term also favored by Lewis.

Tillich and Lewis also found common ground—with each other as well as Eliade—in the deep meaning behind the concept of spiritual epiphany. "Faith as the embracing and centered act of the personality is 'ecstatic.' It transcends both the drives of the nonrational unconscious and the structures of the rational conscious," Tillich wrote. " 'Ecstasy' means 'standing outside of oneself'—without ceasing to be oneself." Lewis explained the experience in strikingly similar language, describing love as having the capacity to make humankind feel as though we are being "taken out of ourselves."

Such blissful moments constitute the joyful, fulfilling life. Becoming attentive to them, seeking them, and experiencing hierophany and ecstasy can spur a change in faith just as easily as a sudden spiritual revelation in the classical sense. And anything of deep personal significance—often experiences suffused with the trappings of memory and bonds of love—can touch this dimension, the rhythms and patterns of art, music, and baseball included. "There are many communities of faith," wrote Tillich, "not only in the religious realm but also in secular culture." Sometimes, touching the transcendent requires a conversion.

Conversion is a serious matter, though it often is trivialized. Over centuries, conquered peoples have "converted" to the conqueror's religion to stay alive. And no true conversion has occurred when one switches Protestant denominations to have an easier commute or to hang with some friends. And so also in baseball.

In the early fifties, Harry Leon Simpson was part of the first generation of African-American players in the major leagues, coming out of his native Georgia through the Negro Leagues and to the Cleveland Indians in 1951. He was a solid, nonspectacular professional in his eight seasons, though Casey Stengel once called him the best defensive right fielder he ever saw. Simpson tied for the league lead in triples twice, knocked in a hundred runs once, played in the World Series for the Yankees, and had a career batting average of .266.

But that's not why he is remembered. In those eight years, he was traded no less than six times, toiling for the Indians, Kansas City, the Yankees, Kansas City again, the White Sox, Pittsburgh, and finally the White Sox again. His peripatetic life got confused with his nickname, Suitcase, though he actually got that after the character in a popular cartoon strip, *Toonerville Trolley*.

Suitcase Simpson played hard, but there is no evidence the venue ever mattered. No conversions occurred; he only wore the uniforms.

By contrast, when pitcher Babe Ruth was sold by the money-grubbing, debt-burdened Red Sox owner Harry Frazee, Ruth promptly not only became an outfielder but became *the* New York Yankee, defining for the future what being a Yankee means. Ruth's famous nickname, the Sultan of Swat, according to several sources, first appeared in *The New York Times* almost at once after he joined his new team. It was not only intended to describe his hitting prowess but also was an alliterative reference to a remote part of present-day Pakistan that was once actually ruled by a sultan. Ruth became royalty; this was a conversion.

Any act of true conversion has at least two major components: dilemma and choice. As the Jesuit Pierre Teilhard de Chardin wrote, "At this crossroads where we cannot stop and wait because we are pushed forward by life—and obliged to adopt an attitude if we want to go on doing anything whatsoever—what are we going freely to decide?" Without attachment, he tells us, we cannot experience detachment.

A student in my class once asked Doris, "Given your experience and knowing what you know now, if it all played out again, would you want the Dodgers to remain in Brooklyn?" At first, the question struck me as ridiculous. Dodgers fans were devastated by the move, an open wound that more than half a century later still pains many in the borough and beyond. Indeed, an old joke in Brooklyn is that if you're trapped in an elevator with Hitler, Stalin, and Walter O'Malley and your gun has only two bullets, what do you do? For Dodgers fans, the answer is clear: Shoot O'Malley twice.

But upon reflection, I realized that the question is profound. As did Doris, who considered the ripple effect. Assuredly, if the Dodgers had stayed, she would not have converted, and therefore she would not have forged the connection with her sons that the Red Sox delivered. The great memories of Red Sox Nation—celebrating dramatic October wins and mourning crushing defeats—would be wiped away. Then, the Dodgers themselves would be seen differently—as today's team rather than as the special team that left (*our* team that left); for the leaving is part of what made New York's golden age of baseball special.

After a long pause, Doris answered.

"No," she said, with equal parts certitude and regret. Then, ever the historian, she added, "The nostalgia and memories are purer this way."

The late Johnny Podres, the pitcher-hero of Game Seven of the 1955 World Series, made a similar point in an interview with Tom. Tom had asked why the tug of that Series' memory remained so very strong.

"One thing you have to keep in mind is what happened that day can never happen again," Podres replied. "There will be other great seventh games, already have been. Someday someone will pitch another perfect game in the Series, someone will make another unassisted triple play, someone will hit another home run to win it all in extra innings. But the Brooklyn Dodgers will never win another championship. They are gone. The events of that day are frozen forever." Like Jeter's records in the Yankee Stadium they now call "old."

And so I say, in unison with my son: "Go Yanks!" With her boys, Doris shouts: "Go Sox!" And Tom exclaims: "Nice catch!"

FIFTH INNING
Miracles

We've all seen teams huddled together during tense moments, praying for a miracle. But those teams are not usually gathered on the side of a highway, their prayers led by a nun.

The story started simply enough. With the contest less than two hours away, we had pulled out of the parking lot of St. Brendan's High School with just enough time to wade through Brooklyn's notorious morning traffic and make it to Archbishop Molloy in Queens for the most important competition of the season.

It was 1961, my first year coaching the St. Brendan's debate team, a role that became a central part of my life over the next fifteen years. We had piled into my 1955 Oldsmobile, known to the students for its worn and torn condition, and affectionately called Betsy. But as I turned onto the Belt Parkway, a cloud of smoke rose from beneath Betsy's hood.

I made my way to examine the engine, glancing back

only to notice that Sister Maria Dolorosa (*sorrowful* in Latin) was leading the girls in prayer, petitioning God to start the car. A few unsuccessful attempts at ignition later, and I, too, became convinced we needed help from a higher authority.

"Sister, you keep praying," I said. "I'm going to get a mechanic."

It was just a joke, but there is a way in which I meant it quite seriously. For me, prayers of petition have always been a futile exercise: "Prayer changes people, not things," I taught my students when I was a professor of religion. The same can be said of miracles—one of the most nuanced notions in the study of religion. To some, a miracle is an answer to prayers—in effect a magic trick from above. But for serious students of religion, a miracle is a special kind of hierophany.

There are, of course, the miracles described in religious legend and myth: Moses parting the Red Sea, Lazarus reclaiming life, and Muhammad splitting the moon to name a few. And there are more personal miracles. But in whatever context it occurs, a miracle is a moment of deep inspiration, emerging from unlikely outcomes at the most crucial times, evoking ecstasy and electricity and awe. The Latin root *miraculum* means "object of wonder." A miracle is another form of hierophany, a manifestation of the divine and a revelation of a wholly different plane.

But "false miracles" abound. Sometimes what appears to be a miracle is, in truth, quite ordinary, the product of coincidence (the rain dance followed by a storm) or even probability.

Probability? Ruma Falk, a professor emeritus of psychology at the Hebrew University of Jerusalem, told a *New York Times* reporter once of the time she traveled to New York over the Rosh Hashanah holiday only to run into a friend from her Israeli neighborhood on a Manhattan street corner. Initially, she felt the encounter was remarkable; but then she recalled that basic statistics teaches that if you have a sufficiently large data set, it is highly probable that there will be specific cases of what might seem improbable. In other words, given the sheer number of visitors to New York from Jerusalem at any given time (especially over the Jewish High Holy Days), it would be more accurate to use the term *miraculous* to describe a day when two people from the same part of Jerusalem *did not* run into each other at a crowded New York intersection. It simply happened, this time, that the good professor was part of the particular pair that met.

By the same rule, though we find it amazing when we share a birthday with somebody else in a relatively small setting, the laws of probability establish that in a room of twenty-three people, there is actually a 50 percent chance that at least two were born on the same day; and in a gathering of fifty-seven people, the likelihood rises to 99 percent. Counterintuitive for most of us, yes; but statistically valid.

Even in baseball, the seemingly "miraculous" often can be explained. But as with religious believers, baseball fans sometimes find statistical and factual explanations less inspiring than the miracle itself.

In 1951, the New York Giants trailed the Brooklyn Dodgers by thirteen and a half games with only a month and a half remaining in the season, a seemingly insurmountable margin. But of their forty-four remaining games, the Giants won thirty-seven, tying the Dodgers and forcing a best-of-three-games playoff. The teams split the first two contests, ensuring that for the first time ever the National League pennant would be decided by the result of a single, winner-take-all playoff game.

As the last half of the last inning of that decisive game began, the Giants trailed 4–1, with their lone run the only one allowed by Dodger pitcher Don Newcombe over a twenty-three-and-two-thirds-inning stretch. But three of the Giants' first four batters reached base, scoring a run and chasing Newcombe from the game. With two men on and one out, the score now 4–2, the Dodgers called upon righty Ralph Branca to face slugger Bobby Thomson, the hero of the first playoff game. Thomson would be followed, if necessary, by a young rookie in the on-deck circle. His name was Willie Mays.

What happened next is baseball lore, known to New Yorkers as the Miracle of Coogan's Bluff (the Manhattan hilltop neighborhood where the Polo Grounds, home field of the Giants, then stood), and known more broadly as the Shot Heard 'Round the World (a phrase that traces back to a Ralph Waldo Emerson poem about the Revolutionary War, but since Branca and Thomson has been linked just as closely to baseball).

More than sixty years later, Thomson's swing still ranks among the most celebrated in baseball history (Francis Ford Coppola used its broadcast in *The Godfather,* even though in real life the game took place a few years after the events of the film). With the count no balls and one strike, Branca delivered a fastball high and inside, and Thomson connected. The result was a hard line drive that left the infield in a hurry but then started losing speed as it carried into the outfield. When Dodgers left fielder Andy Pafko reached the wall 315 feet away, his glove raised high, it was not clear where the ball would land—until Pafko saw it disappear into the seats and into history, its whereabouts unknown to this day.

No less than five Hall of Fame broadcasters announced that game on stations across the country, but the most famous call belonged to Russ Hodges on WMCA-AM, the local Giants station. Don DeLillo's novel *Underworld* opens with a fifty-page description of the moments just before and after Thomson's at-bat, wonderfully capturing the excitement heard in Hodges's voice.

Russ feels the crowd around him, a shudder passing through the stands, and then he is shouting into the mike and there is a surge of color and motion, a crash that occurs upward, stadium-wide, hands and faces and shirts, bands of rippling men, and he is outright shouting, his voice has a power he'd thought long gone—it may lift the top of his head like a cartoon rocket.

He says, *"The Giants win the pennant."*

A topspin line drive. He tomahawked the pitch and the ball had topspin and dipped into the lower deck and there is Pafko at the 315 sign looking straight up with his right arm braced at the wall and a spate of paper coming down.

He says, *"The Giants win the pennant."*

Yes, the voice is excessive with a little tickle of hysteria in the upper register. . . .

He says, *"The Giants win the pennant."*

The crew is whooping. They are answering the roof bangers by beating on the walls and ceiling of the booth. People climbing the dugout roofs and the crowd shaking in its own noise. . . . Russ is shouting himself right out of his sore throat, out of every malady and pathology and complaint and all the pangs of growing up and every memory that is not tender.

He says, *"The Giants win the pennant."*

Four times.

My friend Mike Murray, an avid Giants fan, who owing to a mixture of good fortune and better sense eventually (thirty-three years ago) married my sister, was ecstatic—outside himself, as C. S. Lewis or Paul Tillich would put it, with joy—as Hodges made his call. He plays a tape of the call periodically, and he is still ecstatic each time. Occasionally, he needles the old Dodgers fan in me by supplementing the playing of the tape with a verbatim recitation of Red Smith's recap in the next morning's *New York Herald Tribune*:

"Now it is done. Now the story ends. And there is no way to tell it. The art of fiction is dead. Reality has strangled invention. Only the utterly impossible, the inexpressibly fantastic, can ever be plausible again."

But decades later, Mike and the other remaining New York Giants loyalists were confronted with a startling and unsettling fact: The Giants had cheated. Not only in that game but in home games throughout the last ten weeks of the season, a stretch where the Giants won an astonishing 80 percent of the time. Near the fiftieth anniversary of Thomson's home run, *The Wall Street Journal* reported in detail that the team had used an elaborate signaling system (with a telescope hidden in the clubhouse beyond deep center field and an electric bell-and-buzzer contraption that rang in the bullpen and dugout), which they used to alert Giant hitters to the coming pitches (a single buzz indicated fastball; two meant an off-speed pitch). It was rather sophisticated for the time.

Major League Baseball would not formally codify the rule prohibiting such devices until 1961 (ten years after "The Shot"), but mechanically aided sign-stealing was considered a notorious infraction dating back to 1898 (when a scheme put in place by the Philadelphia Phillies was foiled). To the day he died, Bobby Thomson denied receiving any signals. And my friend Mike Murray denies the turpitude of the act and the significance—even the truthfulness—of what most see as overwhelming evidence. For him, the miraculous moment remains utterly undiminished.

In a provocative little book, *The Myth of the Eternal Return: Cosmos and History*, Mircea Eliade described a scene where a folklorist, Constantin Brailoiu, visits a Romanian village and is regaled with a tragedy of love, a powerful myth *in illo tempore,* a sacred time long ago: A mountain fairy had cast a spell upon a young suitor days before he was to be married and flung him from a cliff. The next day, his body was discovered and brought into town, where his fiancée arranged a funeral full of mythological allusions and liturgical text.

But Brailoiu made an astonishing discovery. The events of the revered story had taken place less than forty years earlier and the heroine was still very much alive. He found her, asked some questions, and heard a very different story: Her fiancée slipped and fell off the cliff on his own and passed away later that same day, after being carried to the village in a last-ditch effort to save his life. The funeral was conducted with the same rituals as was customary at the time; no mention was made of the mountain fairy or any mythological events.

As Eliade wrote,

> Thus, despite the presence of the principal witness, a few years had sufficed to strip the event of all historical authenticity, to transform it into a legendary tale: the jealous fairy, the murder of the young man, the discovery of the dead body, the lament, rich in mythological themes, chanted by the fiancée. Almost all the people of the village had been contemporaries of the authentic historical fact; but this fact, as such, could not satisfy them: the tragic death of a young man on the eve of his marriage was something different from a simple death by accident; it had an occult meaning that could only be revealed by its identification with the category of myth. The mythicization of the accident had not stopped at the creation of a ballad; people told the story of the jealous fairy even when they were talking freely, "prosaically," of the young man's death.

When the folklorist drew the villagers' attention to the authentic version, they replied that the old woman had forgotten; that her great grief had almost destroyed her mind. It was the myth that told the truth: the real story was already only a falsification. Besides, was not the myth truer by the fact that it made the real story yield a deeper and richer meaning, revealing a tragic destiny?

It is a compelling narration. Viewed this way, Mike and his fellow Giants fans, as they ignore the recent discoveries of Giants treachery, are seeking the underlying deeper reality of the matter, in the manner of religious traditions dating back centuries. They focus on the story that actually matters to them. The facts behind the 1951 Giants comeback simply obscure its meaning. For them, Bobby Thomson's home run is miraculous, no matter how it happened.

Every fiber of my Brooklyn Dodger–being screams the same word, *Cheaters!* Four times. You make your own call.

By contrast, there are some baseball miracles about which there is no argument. Each is a tale—be it an individual feat or team performance—of such wonder and consequence that it marks those who behold it, uplifting them. These moments are beyond spectacular. There are background facts and explanations, of course, helpful analyses and crucial contexts, but after all is said and done, the details do not capture the moment.

Miracles in baseball usually change the course of a game, a series, a season. Thus, the most splendid of miracles often occur in September and October, when the games matter most. And the mid-fifties were a miraculous time for the game.

At the top of any list of the spectacular would be three stunning moments in three successive World Series (1954, 1955, and 1956). Each helped produce a championship and memories that have never dulled for the three New York teams: the Giants, the Dodgers, and the Yankees. Two of them unfolded in similar ways; the third is unique to this day.

In 1954, Willie Mays was fresh from two years in the army, but this talented prospect clearly was the Giants' future. A Giant executive once responded to writer Red Smith's query, "How good is this kid Mays?" by saying, "This kid's so good he'll have us eating strawberries in wintertime." That season, Mays had led the team to its first National League pennant since he had been on deck for the Shot Heard 'Round the World three years before. It was the first game of what would be the last Series ever played in the Polo Grounds, and the score was tied 2–2 in the eighth inning. The Giants, huge underdogs, were paired against the Cleveland Indians, winner of 111 games in a 154-game season on the strength of one of the finest pitching staffs ever assembled.

The stage for what is still called "the Catch" was set when the Giant pitcher, Sal Maglie, walked the leadoff batter, center fielder Larry Doby. The next man up, third baseman Al Rosen, singled to deep shortstop; Alvin Dark of the Giants got to the ball but couldn't field it cleanly to make a play. With runners on first and second and nobody out, Giant manager Leo Durocher yanked Maglie and brought in from the bullpen Don Liddle, a decent left-hander with a wicked curveball that could produce ground balls.

The third man up for Cleveland was a respected power hitter who had joined the Indians that summer in a trade with Baltimore, Vic Wertz. Wertz was big, strong, and reliable (he would beat polio two years later). On his way to hitting 266 home runs in a seventeen-year career, he had belted fifteen that season. Liddle got ahead of him, one ball and two strikes, whereupon catcher Wes Westrum signaled for an inside fastball, a tactic designed to set up a curve on the pitch after that.

But the fastball wasn't inside; it was over the plate and Wertz simply crushed it. From the film (and my memory), Wertz did not simply hit a long fly ball, he scorched a line drive directly at Mays, only way over his head (Mays, as usual, was playing relatively shallow in center field). But at the crack of Wertz's bat, Mays turned and took off toward the deepest part of the deepest center field in the major leagues (with a marked distance of nearly five hundred feet). It was a race between Wertz's line drive and one of the fastest players in baseball, with the first game of the Series on the line.

Running at full speed with his back to home plate, Mays sprinted at least fifty yards straight back, running directly at an unpadded wall. In baseball, an over-the-shoulder catch is the most difficult of them all. But as Mays neared the cinder warning track just in front of the wall, he decelerated and stuck out his glove, with his right hand cradling the mitt to form his patented "basket," catching the ball at full extension. The "Say Hey Kid" made the spectacular look routine.

But what he did next was beyond spectacular. Taking no more than three very short steps to balance himself as his hat flew off, he whirled counterclockwise and launched a throw that is remembered today as much as the long run and catch. It traveled more than three hundred feet to Davey Williams of the Giants, who was standing at second base. In the Polo Grounds, runners often tried to advance two bases on long fly balls to center field, but the swift Doby, who had to go back to second to tag up, had no choice but to stop at third as Mays's magnificent throw reached Williams on the fly. With one out, the Giants had a chance to get out of the inning, which they did—after a walk, a critical strikeout, and a routine fly ball.

As with many great baseball moments, this one has a postscript that most people have forgotten: Mays made another magnificent play two innings later at the expense of the same hitter—preventing yet another go-ahead run.

In the tenth inning of the still-tied game, Wertz led off the Cleveland half of the inning against Giants relief pitcher Marv Grissom with another vicious line drive, this time to deep left-center field. Mays took off on another sprint from his position in right-center, this time facing a dilemma, the horns of which were three very difficult choices. He could dive for the fast-moving ball; if he missed, it would roll all the way to the wall some 450 feet away from home plate, in which case Wertz would have an easy triple and possibly an inside-the-park home run. Or he could pass on trying to catch the ball, let it drop, and chase after it as it bounced toward the wall, in which case a triple would be a certainty and the Indians would have the go-ahead run on third base with nobody out. Or he could accelerate his already furious sprint and, stretching his glove hand out as far as he could, attempt to snare the ball as it bounced. He chose the third option, and just barely reached the ball, stopped, and threw a bullet to Hank Thompson at third base while a frustrated Wertz chugged into second base with a four-hundred-foot double. Once again, the Giants had a chance to get out of the inning, and they did.

This set the stage for still another special moment in the bottom of the inning. With one out, Mays and Hank Thompson walked and Durocher decided to pinch-hit for his aging future–Hall of Fame left fielder, Monte Irvin. The substitute batter was anything but a Hall of Famer, a player from Alabama named James Lamar Rhodes, known as Dusty to the baseball world—a decent pinch hitter in the third of his seven major league seasons. Dusty Rhodes hit the first pitch from Cleveland ace Bob Lemon on the fly toward the shortest right field fence in baseball, a mere 258 feet away, and it just barely made the seats, for the three-run home run that won the game. In the ensuing four-game Giants sweep of the stunned Indians, Rhodes hit another home run and batted in fully a third of the twenty-one runs the Giants scored before retreating into obscurity.

One year later, it was the Dodgers who were blessed with a miracle. After having never won a World Series, they led this deciding Game Seven in the sixth inning at Yankee Stadium by the fragile score of 2–0. Dougie and I were not yet at our late-inning post by the radio, crucifix held between us; indeed, we might never have gotten to our post if the Yankee sixth had played out differently.

While Dougie and I played out the final moments of our day in Sister Saint James's eighth-grade class, the Dodgers and pitcher Johnny Podres stared familiar tragedy in the face. The Yankees were at the plate, nobody out, two on base (Billy Martin, who had walked, and Gil McDougald, who beat out a bunt). The next batter was Yogi Berra, as dangerous a clutch hitter as existed in the game and a notorious left-handed pull hitter.

The Dodgers shifted their outfielders several steps toward the right, including left fielder Sandy Amoros, a solid ballplayer who had been discovered in prerevolutionary Cuba four years earlier and who often appeared as a late-inning defensive substitute. Amoros was playing well into left-center field, not too many steps from dead center. But Berra confounded the Dodgers' plans by punching at an outside pitch, sending a towering fly ball down the left field foul line. To some it looked like it was heading foul; to others it looked like a home run; most Dodgers fans simply held their breath. The 2–0 lead was about to evaporate.

Like Mays, Amoros never hesitated before beginning a furious sprint, only he had even farther to go. He ran and he ran while the ball slowly began descending toward the left field corner (a certain run-scoring double). Perhaps five yards from the foul line after his astonishing sprint, Amoros began to decelerate and stretched out his glove. He caught the ball and, in what seemed like one motion, planted his foot, pivoted, and fired a bullet to his relay man, shortstop Pee Wee Reese, more than 150 feet away. Reese, stationed behind third base, himself pivoted as he caught the ball and sent another bullet across the diamond to Gil Hodges at first base. McDougald, thinking that nobody could catch Berra's fly ball, had run all the way past second on the play and was an easy out. The double play saved the game and set the stage for Dougie and me to have a prayerful ninth and for the only Series Brooklyn ever won. The run, the catch, and the throw. Miraculous!

October 8, 1956, also at Yankee Stadium, was and is a unique day in World Series history. A perfect game had not been pitched in any major league game since 1922 and none has been pitched in the Series since that day.

Unlike the sudden, miraculous moments provided by Mays and Amoros, a perfect game builds gradually until— in an instant—it is over, as the last of twenty-seven consecutive batters is retired. It is generally not until at least the sixth inning that its possibility first appears; but from that point on, an excruciating drama unfolds, intensifying with each passing out (indeed, with each passing pitch).

As Don Larsen arrived at the Stadium that day, the Series, again against Brooklyn, was knotted at two victories apiece. He did not know that he was going to start Game Five, only finding out when he discovered a baseball between his spiked shoes (manager Casey Stengel's traditional method of letting his starters know it was their day). The Dodgers had hit him hard the previous year and Larsen had helped the Yankee staff blow a six-run lead in Game Two in 1956, walking four batters in less than two innings of hideous work. In the fourth year of a decidedly unspectacular fourteen-year career, during which he lost more than he won, he had not led the American League in anything, except for his second year, as an Oriole, when he lost twenty-one games.

Larsen had enjoyed a decent 1956, however, winning a career-high eleven games. He was helped by a change in his pitching motion to what was then a novelty, the no-windup delivery. In making the change, he followed the lead of his Yankee and Oriole teammate, Bob Turley. They had come together in 1954 in one of the weirdest trades ever: Over a two-week period, ten Yankees and seven Orioles exchanged uniforms. Larsen was not a bad pitcher, but he never lived up to his potential, in large part due to hard living and heavy drinking.

But on this October day, nothing would stop him, not even the veteran transplant from the hated Giants, Sal Maglie, now pitching for the Dodgers. Each pitcher was perfect through the first three innings—not allowing a single batter to reach first base. The first Yankees hit came in the fourth, a home run by Mickey Mantle. Hank Bauer drove in the second run two innings later with a single.

Larsen, meanwhile, was getting the Dodgers out by locating the ball well and changing speeds more than pitching with power (his seven strikeouts were notable but hardly spectacular). His low pitches produced ground balls, and his high ones became harmless fly balls and pop-ups. Along the way, there were four close calls, but each passed with little notice, because they occurred before the fifth inning had ended and what was possible became apparent.

In the first inning, Pee Wee Reese patiently worked the count to three balls and two strikes before looking at a called third strike. In the second, Jackie Robinson (playing his final games) hit a smash at third baseman Andy Carey that glanced off his glove; it glanced, however, directly over to Gil McDougald at shortstop, who threw out the aging Robinson at first by less than a step (just a few years earlier, Jackie would have had a single).

The key moment came in the fifth inning. With one out, Gil Hodges hit a line drive into deep left-center field.

Running over, Mickey Mantle made a one-handed catch at full gallop for the second out. The next batter, Sandy Amoros, pulled a Larsen fastball deep toward the upper deck in right field, but it curved barely foul at the last instant. After the game, the umpire patrolling right field, veteran Ed Runge, held his right thumb and forefinger an inch apart to show reporters just how close the play really was.

There is, in retrospect, an illusion of inevitability about almost every perfect game, belied by its nail-biting reality. Even so, there is an age-old belief that the surest way to jinx a perfect game is to talk about it. For the last third of the game, the other Yankees followed tradition and ignored Larsen in the dugout. On the air, the Dodgers' legendary announcer, Vin Scully, avoided the dreaded words while doing the play-by-play with his customary professionalism. The only player known to have broken the unwritten rule, ironically, was Larsen himself, who earned more than one rebuke down the stretch from teammates by wondering aloud if he could really do it.

He could. The final out, a called third strike by umpire Babe Pinelli on pinch hitter Dale Mitchell, was only the ninety-seventh pitch Larsen threw that day. You could break down each of them and still fail to grasp Larsen's achievement. The picture of Yogi Berra jumping into Larsen's arms on the mound immediately after that last out is one of the most reproduced photos in baseball history. The ecstatic joy it conveys is at once transforming and elevating.

The miraculous is the grist of myth; and myth permeates religion. Sometimes the story of a miracle entails the intervention or manifestation of a higher power: Yahweh's message reaching Moses at the burning bush; the angelic revelation before Hagar in the desert; Krishna teaching Arjuna in the Bhagavad Gita. But always the miracle conveys a wonderment and amazement that transports one to what Eliade called "a place that is sacred above all."

So too in baseball. Just before the end of a roller-coaster 1991 season, the Minnesota Twins' popular, fundamentals-fixated manager, Tom Kelly, observed with atypical enthusiasm, "This is a storybook. Each chapter is a game and each game is better than the last." Kelly's wonderment was justified. By October, his Twins were one World Series game away from the most improbable championship ever, a phoenix-like resurrection, from last the year before to Game Seven of what many baseball people consider the best World Series of them all—a Series made of the stuff from which hierophanies and stories of the miraculous arise.

The Twins were the first team ever to have gone from dead last to first the very next season; however, the Twins' momentary status as baseball's only phoenix did not last. Just six days after Minnesota secured its first-place finish, the Atlanta Braves finished an eight-game winning streak and edged out the Los Angeles Dodgers on the penultimate day of the season to become the second team to have moved from last to first. When the two teams met in the World Series, they were the first two worst-to-first teams to face each other for the championship of any major professional sport; and it hasn't come close to happening since then.

It was fitting that the World Series was an epic affair—the kind that accentuates the importance of every pitch and play. It was a blend of exhilaration and anxiety, of motion and rest that is possible only in a sport without a clock: Pitch by pitch, the percentages and strategy change. A runner, an out, the inning, the score, the matchups—all part of a complex formula unfolding in slow motion until, in a flash, a move is made, and an equally complex ballet begins as the intensity grows. A sport without a clock.

Of the seven games, five were decided by a lone run, four of those in the winning team's last time at bat. And Game Seven was an extra-inning cliff-hanger, decided by the only run scored in the game after as heroic a pitching performance as the Series has ever seen by a grizzled veteran who both willed and expected victory. For the victorious Twins, the deciding game was the second extra-inning win in as many nights.

The popular TV highlight of the Twins' 1990 cellar-dwelling season was a July day in Boston when they pulled off two triple plays in the same game, each a 'round-the-horn, third-to-second-to-first improbability; in reality, the highlight of that failed season was a set of shrewd off-season moves that quietly set the stage for the miraculous season of 1991. They let a beloved veteran, Gary Gaetti, go and found a cheaper replacement at third base in a human spark plug named Mike Pagliarulo. They outbid others for slugger Chili Davis. They promoted from the minor leagues two of their best prospects, pitcher Scott Erickson (who would win twenty games in 1991, his first full season) and second baseman Chuck Knoblauch (the 1991 Rookie of the Year). But above all, they obtained St. Paul native Jack Morris, a ferociously competitive pitcher who had led the Detroit Tigers to a championship seven years before and who, the following year, would be a key cog in the Toronto Blue Jays' breakout season.

The dramatic effect of these moves was apparent as the 1991 season unfolded. Team spirit was high: Several team members recorded a dance video and others recorded a team song to the tune of Beethoven's Ninth Symphony. The team had a very strong first half and never relinquished first place after claiming it in mid-July, finishing eight games ahead of the White Sox and then cruising past Toronto in the playoffs to reach the World Series.

Atlanta's transformation was more laborious. In 1990, their highlight was a new manager appointed midway through the season, Bobby Cox. The choice of Cox was interesting because he made it himself (as the team's general manager). As he returned to a position he had held in the eighties, no one could have known he was on the verge of an unprecedented fourteen consecutive division titles, several postseason heart-breakers, but one memorable world championship in 1995.

Cox made few changes to his young team as 1991 began. And at first the team was mediocre. There was, however, a young, talented pitcher named John Smoltz who had grown up in Michigan idolizing Morris. A fourteen-game winner in 1990, Smoltz began the season distracted by his wife's pregnancy: He lost eleven of his first thirteen decisions, then he and the team stabilized and ignited. Smoltz won twelve of his next fourteen decisions, while the team's record after the All-Star Game was a dominant fifty-five wins against just twenty-eight losses. What would become Cox's trademark emphasis on pitching began to pay off in the playoffs as well: The Braves won an exciting seven-game series against the Pittsburgh Pirates, with a young Steve Avery winning two 1–0 shutouts and Smoltz notching victories in the other two, including a 4–0 shutout in Game Seven.

The World Series was spectacular in every sense. Atlanta had a chance to win it when the Series shifted back to Minneapolis for Game Six, a nail-biter that was tied after the Braves batted in the top of the eleventh inning. In the Minnesota dugout, the first man due up, All-Star center fielder Kirby Puckett, told Chili Davis he was going to try to bunt his way on base against Brave reliever Charlie Leibrandt. "Bunt my ass," replied Davis. "Hit it out and let's go home." (Foreshadowing Derek Jeter–to–Aaron Boone twelve years later.) Puckett did precisely that. The picture of his joyous arm-pumping trot is memorialized today in a statue outside the Twins' new ballpark.

The next night belonged to Morris. Matched against Smoltz, the two pitchers each produced scoreless master-pieces that masked the tension in the dugouts. After the seventh inning, Kelly kept asking the aging Morris if he wanted to call it quits; Morris answered with cold stares and head shakes.

After Morris recorded the third out in the Braves' half of the tenth inning on his 126th pitch of the night (astonishingly, his 320th of the Series), the victory came with sudden decisiveness: a double, a sacrifice bunt, and two intentional walks to the team's sluggers (Puckett and Kent Hrbek) by a relief pitcher (Alejandro Pena) who preferred facing light-hitting Jarvis Brown. Kelly scoured his depleted bench for a pinch hitter, focusing only on an injured Gene Larkin for the bases-loaded, one-out opportunity. Larkin delivered on the first pitch, a sharp hit into left field that ended the game, the Series, and a miraculous season—and sending fans in the Metrodome into a raucous frenzy.

For fans with long memories and a sense of history, the sudden ascent of Atlanta in 1991 echoed an earlier Series, with a happier ending for the Braves—a Series that caused the word *miracle* to be affixed to a team for the first time.

Before coming to Atlanta in 1966, the Braves had been in Milwaukee, and before 1953, they had been one of the charter National League teams as the Boston Braves. The team had emerged as the Boston Red Stockings in the 1870s and were next the Red Caps, the Beaneaters, the Doves, and then the Rustlers. They became the Braves in 1912 because one of their owners, ex–New York cop James Gaffney, was a fixture of the Tammany Hall political machine and Tammany's famous symbol had long been an American Indian.

Whatever their name, the Braves were terrible, losing an average of ninety-eight times a season for the first decade after the National and American Leagues were joined while their American League counterparts, the Red Sox, were flourishing. And then it happened, what *The New York Times* would label in a midcentury review the greatest upset in sports history to that point. A new manager helped—George Stallings, a tempestuous motivator and a pioneer in shuffling players in and out of lineups (what we know as platooning). Stallings needed to platoon because he had no first-class hitters. His players were known for their fielding—second baseman Johnny Evers, near the end of his career six years after he helped the Cubs win it all, and a very young, very small shortstop named Walter James Vincent "Rabbit" Maranville, in the third of what would become twenty-three Hall of Fame seasons.

The team began 1914 with characteristic incompetence, losing twenty-eight of its first forty games. They were in last place as late as July 18, eleven games behind the New York Giants. Legend has it that a clubhouse tirade by Johnny Evers ignited the team—a tirade prompted after the team lost a doubleheader to Brooklyn and traveled to Buffalo to play an exhibition game, only to get crushed by a minor league team.

For their final 86 games that year, the Braves' record was an astonishing 67-19. Pitching was central, as three otherwise forgettable pitchers had career years. "Seattle" Bill James, who would disappear after just four seasons, won twenty-six, as did Richard "Baldy" Rudolph, while George "Lefty" Tyler won sixteen. They caught the Giants after Labor Day, winning a three-game series (attended by nearly one hundred thousand amazed fans) that included a victory over the legendary Christy Mathewson. At this point, the Braves had so captured the town's fancy that the haughty Red Sox lent them their new ballpark and the Braves left their tiny home in the city's South End for Fenway.

The climax of the surge was the September 9 game against the Phillies. The Braves had a pitcher who had reported late each spring for a few years because he was a student at Harvard Law School. George "Iron" Davis had been persuaded that spring by Stallings to learn the still-legal spitball. Against the Phillies, with the Braves clinging to a one-game lead in the pennant race, Davis threw a no-hitter for one of his three victories that year (he won seven in his career). After that, the Braves never looked back.

But they were huge underdogs as they approached the World Series against the Philadelphia Athletics, managed by owner Cornelius McGillicuddy—or Connie Mack as he eventually preferred. The Athletics were among the elite. The team featured two future Hall of Fame hitters (Eddie Collins and Frank "Home Run" Baker) and three future Hall of Fame pitchers (Eddie Plank, Herb Pennock, and Charles Albert "Chief" Bender). The Athletics were so stocked with talent and Connie Mack was so tight with his money that he passed on a young pitcher that year who was being shopped by his minor league team in Baltimore; instead, Babe Ruth signed with the Red Sox.

Before the World Series, Chief Bender was so confident and cocky that he refused to read the scouting report on the Braves, saying it was beneath him to worry about "some bush league team." In the first game, the Braves clobbered him, 7–1. They followed that victory by winning the next three games, completing the first sweep in the young World Series' history.

Baseball miracles can happen anywhere, of course. They are not the sole property of the World Series or even of the major leagues. I was reminded of this in March of 2011 as I read reports of the hideous earthquake and tsunami that devastated much of northern Japan, killing thousands. In the aftermath of the disaster, a high school team from the region decided to keep playing in a national tournament on borrowed fields far from their home; their decision caught the country's attention. According to newspaper accounts, they had survived the tsunami because they were practicing on a field high above their town, which was destroyed; indeed, the players helped evacuate patients from a nearby nursing home during the disaster.

One of the young players, Toshiki Onodera, explained his team's decision: "We were playing baseball and we were all together when the tsunami happened. We were saved. Now I think baseball is helping to save us again."

Added his proud father: "Our family, we lost everything. We lost three cars, two fishing boats, all the machinery to cultivate rice. Assets, they mean nothing now. But for my son, baseball still matters. Joy is more important than materials."

For me, this story reflected the spirit in my own city after the tragic events of September 11, 2001. In the weeks that followed, baseball bolstered a still-reeling America. It helped that New York's Yankees (the reigning champions as a result of beating the Mets the year before) were central to the postseason drama.

Three World Series games that year will always be remembered for their stunning drama and surprise endings; but we (my son and I) sensed that something special was happening even before the Series began. The clearest signal was a unique play in the divisional playoffs between the Yankees and Oakland. If Game One in 1954 featured "the Catch" by Mays, then Game Three of this Division Series featured "the Flip." The hero was the consummate Yankee of this period, shortstop Derek Jeter.

With Oakland up 2–0 in the series and needing just one more win to send the Yankees home, the game was a pitchers' duel between Mike Mussina of the Yankees and the A's Barry Zito. The Yankees led 1–0 on a home run by catcher Jorge Posada. With two outs in the bottom of the seventh inning, Jeremy Giambi singled to right field.

The next batter, Terrence Long, promptly ripped a ball down the right field line, and Giambi, a notoriously slow runner, took off as the ball bounced toward the corner. Approaching third base, he was waved home by the coach, Ron Washington. The careful observer of baseball is rewarded in moments like this (an extra-base hit with men on base), as an intricate ballet unfolds: In this case, as right fielder Shane Spencer raced to field the ball before it could reach the wall, Mussina moved to back up third base; second baseman Alfonso Soriano positioned himself in short right field as the relay man; and first baseman Tino Martinez located himself on a line with Soriano closer to home plate.

Jeter was where shortstops go in this elaborate dance—close to the pitcher's mound, ready to do one of three things: cut off a throw toward third base, cover second in the event of a play on the hitter, or, least likely, move to get any errant throw from Spencer.

When Spencer's throw sailed over Soriano's head, over Martinez's, and bounced toward the A's on-deck circle, Jeter raced toward the first base line, fielded the ball with two hands at the line, and with his bare hand flipped the ball sideways twenty feet to Posada, who tagged Giambi, whose right foot was in midair over home plate.

We must be careful about using the word *never* when it comes to baseball; that said, a second play like Jeter's has yet to be identified, let alone one at such a pivotal moment. Such moments in baseball—and though this particular *play* is unique, this kind of *moment* occurs regularly—can be described, but the sublime experience the moment evokes cannot be captured in words; in that moment the beholder lives beyond words. Once the amazement had abated, the Yankees sailed into the World Series; but the autumn of 2001 was far from finished.

The three classic games in the World Series against the Arizona Diamondbacks—Games Four, Five, and Seven—live in lore with the seven played by Minnesota and Atlanta ten years before.

Game Four: Bottom of the ninth inning, Yankees trailing in the Series two games to one, Arizona leading 3–1. Diamondback reliever Byung-Hyun Kim, at twenty-two, becomes the first Korean-born player to appear in the World Series. After striking out the side in the eighth, he gives up a one-out single to Paul O'Neill. With two outs, Tino Martinez crushes Kim's first pitch into the right-center field bleachers to tie the game. The very next inning, Derek Jeter wins the game with another home run off Kim, this one on a full-count pitch, mere moments after the clock atop the center field scoreboard strikes midnight, ushering in November baseball for the very first time.

Game Five: Again, the bottom of the ninth inning. Again, Arizona leading by two runs. Again, Kim is pitching in relief. Again, the Yankees are down to their very last out with one runner on base, after a leadoff double by Posada. This time, Kim hangs a slider to third baseman Scott Brosius, who promptly puts it in the left field seats to tie the game. The Yankee victory comes in the twelfth, with Soriano knocking in ex-Twin Chuck Knoblauch with a single.

To this day, I can feel the cheers coursing through my body and recall the joy. Pure amazement. Awe. *Mysterium tremendum et facscinans*. To me, a miracle.

I remember how the Diamondbacks' infielders raced to the mound to console a disconsolate Kim (the New York tabloids the next day carried a full-page picture of the dejected pitcher crouched in agony on the mound). This wasn't merely the Yankees or New York post-9/11. This was baseball. Heartbreaking to some, even as it creates joy for others. And it wasn't over yet.

Game Seven: After Arizona, back in Phoenix, erupted to crush the Yankees 15–2 in Game Six, the stage was set for a special ending. Mike Murray and I could taste a Yankee victory and had decided to suggest that the victory parade in New York's concrete canyons should reverse its traditional route, beginning uptown and ending (this year only) at Ground Zero.

Roger Clemens, still an ace at thirty-nine and completing

his eighteenth season, would face the Diamondbacks' ace, thirty-four-year-old Curt Schilling—starting his third game of the Series and pitching his three hundredth inning of the season, his fourteenth, on just three days' rest. Schilling stayed in perhaps one inning too long as Soriano hit a solo home run in the eighth to break a 1–1 tie. Yankee manager Joe Torre immediately brought in the mighty Mariano Rivera to attempt a two-inning save.

Rivera struck out the side in the bottom of the eighth (shades of Kim), yielding only a single. But after Randy Johnson, the other Diamondback ace (who, after his victory in Game Six, was giving the team four outs of relief while pitching on no rest), retired the Yankees in the ninth, the roof caved in. It is still a maddening blur for me: a single by Mark Grace, an off-target throw to second by Rivera on a bunt by Damian Miller, an accurate throw to third by Rivera on a bunt by Jay Bell to get Grace, a Tony Womack double to right to even the score, and then a bad pitch by Rivera (his only one) that hit Craig Counsell to load the bases.

The next batter, slugger Luis Gonzalez, then hit as weak and soft a line drive as has ever been hit (a "dying quail," as such hits are sometimes called) over the head of Derek Jeter, just far enough to make it to the outfield grass. Had the Yankees not been drawn in—hoping to force out the potential winning run at home plate—it would have been the most routine of catches. Instead, it scored Bell with the Series-winning run.

In baseball, some of the most solid hits become line drive outs and some of the weakest become box score hits; a few even win games. There are other times when players accomplish precisely what their team needs, only to see their own statistics diminished as a result; and times when they fail in their objective yet are rewarded—on paper or, even better, on the scoreboard. In religion, this is the idea of concupiscence— to be a saint, authorities do not require a lifetime of perfection. Rivera on this night, like Eckersley and his brethren of Hall of Fame relievers in autumns past, surely can relate. And so the human condition is reflected in this sport as in no other. Here, in the shadow of national tragedy and subsequent recovery, baseball stirred the nation's soul.

The Yankees had lost. There would be no victory parade through the concrete canyons. But that night in November, the latest a World Series had ever ended—because play had been suspended for several days after 9/11—baseball and its fans were treated to a miraculous game, and at just the right moment.

There is a tacit—on occasion explicit—acceptance that some feats by individuals or teams in a game or over an entire season or in a World Series simply cannot be explained. We are left only to shake our heads in wonder, to exult, to accept the simple fact that Willie Mays and Sandy Amoros caught those fly balls and that the 1914 Braves won the World Series, and having accepted the fact, to marvel at the miracle (and how, in the midst of our ordinary days, the moment stands apart and reveals something to us).

In religion, miracles also play an important role. In John's New Testament, Jesus Christ observed that "unless you people see signs and wonders, you will never believe." And yet He also celebrates those faithful who have never seen Him, avowing that "blessed are they who have not seen yet believe."

For his part, Thomas Jefferson, good Deist that he was, attempted an analysis of the New Testament in retirement, purging it of all references to the supernatural or miraculous. The result, many scholars have since agreed, was a rehash of garden-variety moral philosophizing that is missing any spark, much less a sign or a wonder.

In the Hebrew Scriptures, on many occasions God speaks and acts like a participant in the thrilling narrative, using miraculous works to reward humans who do good and punish those who are not observant or who do evil. And yet many Jewish scholars are cognizant of the contradiction between the belief that God's creation is perfect and stories of His episodic interventions in worldly affairs to correct mistakes. Some argue that everything, literally, was set in motion at creation, that God created the natural world to shield Himself from man, to force man to discover or fail to discover faith.

In Islam, Muhammad was no miracle worker and indeed rejected entreaties to perform miracles, insisting according to Muslim scholars that the Koran itself is the miracle; and yet the stories of his life are replete with miraculous acts. So also Buddhism, built as it is on rigorous self-effacement, rejects miracles as a general matter; Buddhists aspire to *om mani padre hum,* a mantra that means "jewel in the lotus," referring to finding nirvana (the jewel) in life (the lotus of the universe)—a self-journey through the "gateless gate" of Zen. Its literature, however, contains stories of Buddha himself walking on water and of monks who achieve states where they can levitate or become invisible.

In the end, however, the great traditions acknowledge that the divine is by definition beyond the capacity of a human to fathom, that faith is not certainty, that room must be left for wonder at the ineffable. This is the place from which miracles arise.

Chet Raymo, in his book *When God Is Gone Everything Is Holy,* discussed how we might approach these miraculous moments. He said there are two pathways. The first, which he notes is the one followed by an overwhelming majority of people all over the world in all historical periods, "looks for God in exceptional events" and reflects "the human predilection for the supernatural," a desire to see an active God filling the gaps in our knowledge as well as literally performing miraculous feats.

"It is easy to understand why the God of the gaps is so

popular," wrote Raymo. "By looking for God in our ignorance, we can make him in our own image, call him Father,
speak to him as friend, claim a personal relationship, count
on his intervention in our lives. It is a consoling thought to
think that the creator of the universe—those hundreds of
billions of galaxies—has me, yes *me*, as the apple of his eye."

Raymo offers a second path, however, one that embraces mystery and wonder. He correctly associates this
path with the earliest Christian mystics like Saint Columba-
nus, who wrote: "Who shall examine the secret depths of
God? Who shall dare to treat of the eternal source of the
universe? Who shall boast of knowing the infinite God,
who fills all and surrounds all, who enters into all and passes
beyond all, who occupies all and escapes all?"

Nikos Kazantzakis (who also gave us *Zorba the Greek*)
described this force as "the dread essence beyond logic."
For those who enjoy Latin, this is *Deus Absconditus,* the
God of mystery, whom Raymo calls "the hidden God who
is not this and is not that, who evades all names and metaphors, even the pronouns 'who' and 'he,' Rudolph Otto's
mysterium tremendum et fascinans. It is not a God with
whom we can have a personal relationship or who attends
our personal needs. It is a God we approach through the
valley of shadow and the dark night of the soul, who al-
ways hides just beyond our reach."

Vic Wertz's fly ball falls into Willie Mays's glove. Johnny
Podres throws nine shutout innings on October 4, 1955.
These miraculous, ineffable events are true hierophanies of
a baseball life. Explanation and analysis can't begin to do
them justice.

And it simply is the case that on one day, a perfectly
ordinary person, a sinner named Don Larsen, pitched a
perfect game in the World Series. No one can truly explain
his feat, which is why it remains so wondrous more than
half a century later.

The Atlanta Braves were one out away from defeat in yet another World Series when their mercurial manager, Bobby Cox, finally ran out of signs to flash to his players. All he could muster was a deep sigh and a cold, blank stare toward the pitcher's mound.

Cox had been there before—three of his previous four trips to the Series had ended in bitter disappointment—but this one, in 1999, felt different. For the first time since their captivating run of division and league championships had begun nearly a decade earlier, the mighty Braves were about to be swept four games to none. Cox had already decided to decline the post-Series interview with NBC—another first. He would send star pitcher John Smoltz in his place.

Elsewhere in the dugout, Cox's third baseman and that season's Most Valuable Player in the National League, Chipper Jones, also was scanning the Yankee Stadium scene. He had a different reaction; he simply shook his head and started to laugh. Moments earlier he had seen the Braves' powerful first baseman, Ryan Klesko, break three bats in a single turn at the plate, the last one shattering as he produced a meek pop fly to second base. Klesko then trotted back to join the rest of his teammates in watching their season end with a whimper.

What the Braves also were watching was greatness. There was simply no answer for Mariano Rivera's cut fastball. When the game finished, Jones compared the pitch to "a buzz saw."

The Yankees' closer had discovered his cutter by accident two years earlier, in 1997, while tossing a ball to another reliever in the bullpen. After initially trying to change his mechanics to straighten out the pitch (when gripped correctly, it resembles a four-seam fastball but is held slightly off-center, with the thumb toward the inside of the ball, causing it to break, or cut, toward a right-handed pitcher's glove side as it reaches home plate), Rivera decided to embrace it, and the game of baseball has never been the same. By 2011, *Sports Illustrated* estimated that a quarter of all major league starters regularly used the pitch as part of their repertoire. But no pitcher, starter or reliever, throws it as skillfully as Rivera.

With a week remaining in the 2011 season, Rivera threw twelve cutters in thirteen pitches to retire the Minnesota Twins' batters in order and earn his record-breaking 602nd career save. James Traub, my dear friend who for several years joined me in teaching the Baseball as a Road to God seminar at NYU, wrote in *The New York Times Magazine:* "Rivera, when pressed, attributes his gifts to providence; people of a more secular bent say that he combines one of the single greatest pitches the game has ever seen—his cutter—with an inner calm, and a focus, no less unusual and no less inimitable."

That inner calm, indispensable in a closer, traces back to the shores of Puerto Caimito, Panama, a fishing village that counted Rivera, his parents, and his three siblings among its thousand or so residents in the seventies. "Life was simple," he remembers.

Rivera was born into poverty but remembers his childhood more for the many gatherings of his tight-knit family and long, baseball-filled days. Tree branches (the straighter, the better, Rivera said) or sticks found lying in the street served as bats; makeshift balls were created by wrapping fishing nets with tape. Rivera's glove was fashioned from a flattened-out milk carton or, sometimes, part of a cardboard box. "It had to fit in your back pocket," he once told a reporter, recalling how in the days before he pitched in baseball's grand coliseums, he considered that cardboard glove as "beautiful as a major league glove."

Shortly after Rivera's record-breaking game against the Twins, Sweeny Murti, a local radio reporter who has covered the Yankees for years, asked him if he had allowed himself a small moment to revel in his achievement—his long journey from, quite literally, sandlot to superstardom. Rivera, a deeply pious man who plans someday to be a minister, did not consider it an achievement but a "blessing," he said. "From the mercy of God." Maybe so.

"I have always said that you cannot be a major league baseball player unless you have been touched by the hand of God. Period." So said the never-doubting Tippy (of the Stottlemyre and Wilhelm questions) in a spontaneous soliloquy on the game. "Baseball players are born, not made; you cannot turn someone into a major league baseball player unless he was touched." Here he reminds me of Michael Jordan's failed attempt to transform himself from a great basketball star to a successful professional baseball player.

"What's more," Tippy continued, "even those who have been touched have to hone their talents every single day. There are those who have had the gift but have squandered it." He lists Joe Pepitone of the Yankees, Lou Johnson of the LA Dodgers, and Richie Allen of the Phillies. They were accomplished ballplayers, but they never achieved the super-stardom for which they once seemed destined.

"Allen is the most egregious case," he said. "He could have been one of the eight or ten greatest ever, but he just did not do the work. He once hit two inside-the-park homers in one game. Nobody has done that but him." I decided not to challenge him. He continued: "Yet he never made it big."

Tippy concluded: "What makes baseball so great is that everybody can play it—little kids and old people. But only the blessed are destined to play in the majors."

We often speak of a blessed ballplayer in the sense that Rivera and Tippy use the term. And the word *blessing* is used in many other ways and contexts, both religious and secular.

There are those blessed folks who walk through life (or a baseball season) with a special light shining upon them—in baseball terms, teams of destiny like Tug McGraw's 1973 Mets.

There are those times when what are called in religion "prayers of petition" are believed to have been answered with a blessing, as when a batter gets a hit after crossing himself or, conversely, when the same batter strikes out with the bases loaded after a fan of the pitcher entreats his God.

Or there is the blessing of a magnificent catch or clutch home run, attributed perhaps to an intervening deity, as witness the fingers pointing skyward after a play, or the locker room "Thank you, Jesus" for a fortuitous result, or even a more general gratitude for good fortune, like Joe DiMaggio's thanking the Almighty for making him a Yankee. In this regard, a blessing is a function of our belief that, in some way, "God is on our side," with all the evident tensions such a statement entails once we realize that "they" (the fans on the other side) are invoking a God as well (often the same God).

My focus, however, is on a particular, profound meaning of blessing—as an experience deeply connected to its sibling, the curse. The two phenomena have a special synergy. As I use the word, *blessing* is the ecstatic sensation one experiences after being released from profound accursedness. In this sense, blessings and curses are more than countervailing forces; they are as inextricably intertwined as are faith and doubt. To be relieved of a curse is to experience fully and completely a blessing.

To be accursed is very personal. The Latin root *ad*, which gives force to the simple word *curse*, means that the curse sticks "to" its object; thus the blessing (the relief) also is deeply personal. All this plays easily into baseball, characterized as it is by slow, intense rhythms.

The great baseball curses are associated with painful, prolonged championship droughts, booted ground balls, dropped third strikes, and most of all, wrenching defeats. They are tied in legend to events off the field, stories of the bizarre (involving a black cat, a billy goat, and a Broadway show) that in retrospect are seen as omens and harbingers.

Three stand out, involving teams whose identities are deeply tied to how they and their fans have dealt with accursedness and epic adversity—the Brooklyn Dodgers, the Boston Red Sox, and the Chicago Cubs. What matters, as it turns out, is not so much the story behind the curse as the way the teams, towns, and fans handle it. Those reactions run the gamut, from the defiant persistence of hope to the cynical scapegoating of despair to the almost cheerful acceptance of disappointment. Hope, despair, or resignation. The reaction to accursedness is key; and that reaction, in the end, shapes the blessing when and if it comes, and determines its effect.

For a wonderful example of Oscar Wilde's witty description of second marriages (a triumph of hope over experience), the first place to turn is that sprawling agglomeration of urban villages east of Manhattan called Brooklyn, which (perhaps ironically) was once known as the

Borough of Churches. Brooklyn native and later Ohio State professor David Neal Miller has described the borough's diverse collection of two dozen neighborhoods as the "cradle of tough guys, Nobel laureates, fourth-largest city in the United States, proof of the power of marginality, and homeland of America's most creative diasporic culture."

It is not known just how the famous cry—Wait'll Next Year—originated. Most likely, it came from ordinary people and simply spread (the way things go viral in today's Internet age) until it was a headline and then a mantra. After all the end-of-season and World Series agonies between 1941 and 1954, some soothing aphorism surely was needed. Some comfort was needed, for example, after the Dodgers missed a chance to tie the Phillies on the last day of the season in 1950 because the potential winning run (in the person of outfielder Cal Abrams) was thrown out by a mile at home plate, or after Bobby Thomson's three-run home run in the bottom of the ninth inning the very next year ended an epic two-month slide.

Angry fingers were pointed at the third base coach (Milt Stock) who waved Cal Abrams toward home. And pitcher Ralph Branca was hanged in effigy from several streetlights in Brooklyn on the horrible night after he threw the fat fastball that Thomson hit. But as in the years before, anger soon became hope, "next year" being just around the corner. And so "the faithful," as Dodgers fans were called, affirmed the power of the great virtue of hope and rejected the deadly sin of despair and the ugliness it produces.

And that spirit of hope endured against all manner of tribulations. In the 1952 World Series against the Yankees, the Dodgers' majestic first baseman, Gil Hodges, went a horrid 0 for 21 in seven games, a famous slump that continued into the following spring. Not a single boo was aimed in his direction during his ordeal. This Indiana coal miner's son was cherished by Brooklyn for much more than his hitting and fielding; so it was no surprise that on an unseasonably steamy Sunday, a priest named Herbert Redmond announced to his congregation: "It's far too hot for a sermon. Keep the Commandments and say a prayer for Gil Hodges." The point is not that Hodges started hitting again shortly thereafter (though he did); the point is that the prayers were offered.

Therein lies the larger meaning: Being a kid and a Dodgers fan in that golden era was to be part of something larger than one's self. This is the essence of Saint Paul's trinity of blessedness—faith, hope, and love. Of course, Cal Abrams should have been held at third base, and, of course, Ralph Branca should not have entered the game, let alone thrown Thomson the same fastball in almost the same location twice; but we never stopped praying for Cal, for Ralph, for Gil, and for the Dodgers. Faith, hope, and love. Wait'll next year.

In a way, repeating that mantra or praying for Gil Hodges might have illustrated the popular definition of insanity: repeating the same action over and over while expecting a different result. But somehow we knew that to be accursed—repeatedly to suffer inexplicable but apparently preordained pain or hardship—was a necessary prelude to being released from its clutches and receiving great (and all the more enjoyable) blessings.

A deeply religious man, Hodges did not bemoan his slump or search for scapegoats or even give up hope and self-indulgently claim virtue in bearing humiliation gracefully. He grasped the inevitability of slumps even as he maintained his determination to improve and overcome. He, like all of Brooklyn, answered accursedness with faith and hope. And he, like Brooklyn, ultimately was blessed.

What is today the most famous of all the curses in baseball evoked a very different response from those it afflicted. So slow was this curse to build that it was not even discovered by its victims until roughly seventy years after the event that (it is said) precipitated it. Such, however, is the odd nature of the Curse of the Bambino, the damning of the Boston Red Sox and owner Harry Frazee for the sale in early 1920 of Babe Ruth to the New York Yankees.

Memories dim or are erased by time, but the story of Babe Ruth's departure is much more interesting than its typically shorthand retelling, and it shows that curses are never simple things. And I should note that its telling here is colored by the fact that for a Yankees fan, the Sox are *the* enemy. One person's saints are often another's sinners; or put differently, there are differing histories of the Crusades, or of the arrival of Cortés in Mexico. Perspective matters.

Baseball always has had bizarre, flamboyant, roguish owners, but at the end of the twentieth century's second decade, the Red Sox had the misfortune to be owned by one of the most outlandish, Harry Frazee. Frazee was leveraged to the limits of his finances; and he was a producer of theatrical extravaganzas on what was becoming known simply as Broadway. After 1918, his Red Sox sat atop the baseball world, the winners of five of the first fifteen World Series and boasting the finest pitching staff in the major leagues, anchored by the still-young southpaw Babe Ruth, whose batting potential already was well-known. In 1919, Sox manager Ed Barrow began to wean Ruth from pitching. Ruth won nine games in 1919, but (playing in the outfield) he batted .322, drove in 114 runs, and broke the then-record for home runs with the astonishing total of twenty-nine (more than the total of ten of the fifteen other major league teams).

Strapped for cash, Frazee began to dismantle the team that July, when he sent one of his star pitchers, Carl Mays, to the Yankees for two journeymen and forty thousand dollars. Mays was on his way to a two-hundred-plus-victory career and would be the ace of the Yankees' first pennant-winning team in 1921, with twenty-seven wins. The Ruth outrage occurred on January 3, 1920. No Yankees came north as compensation, just $125,000 for Frazee plus a

$300,000 loan secured by Fenway Park itself (meaning, oddly enough, the first ballpark the Yankees "owned" was that of their rival's, fully three years before opening their own palace in the Bronx). And the disgraceful episodes continued at the end of that year, when an eight-player deal with the Yankees could not mask the transfer of another expensive Red Sox pitcher, Waite Hoyt. Hoyt went on to the Hall of Fame and was the ace of New York's fabled 1927 juggernaut. Nor were the Red Sox quite finished even then; in 1923, their last star pitcher, Herb Pennock, went to the Yankees and eventually the Hall of Fame for three more nobodies and fifty thousand more dollars. Legend has it Frazee needed all that money to finance a lavish production called *No, No, Nanette*. The legend is not literally true, but what is true is that money was the root of all this evil.

Obscured in this madness was the fact that Ed Barrow himself read Frazee's handwriting on the wall and departed for the Yankees after 1920. In New York, Barrow developed the modern, crucial baseball position of general manager and for the next quarter century was the actual architect of the dynasty that won fourteen pennants and ten World Series during his tenure, eventually landing him a spot in the Hall of Fame.

For the decade following Frazee's fire sale, the Red Sox languished in or near the cellar until they were bought in 1933 by Thomas Austin Yawkey, the adopted son of a Michigan industrialist (actually his uncle, at one point the owner of the Detroit Tigers), who paid $1.5 million out of his $40 million inheritance to buy the team the instant he was legally able to start spending it. Yawkey was dedicated to baseball, sank millions into the team and Fenway Park, and slowly built a competitive collection of players, helped immeasurably by the discovery of a talented kid from San Diego named Ted Williams. The Sox won a pennant in 1946 but suffered a heartbreaking seventh-game loss to the Cardinals in the World Series; they came achingly close to Cleveland and the Yankees in the pennant races of the late forties; after a seventeen-year string of mediocrity, and worse, they secured the Impossible Dream pennant in 1967, only to lose another seven-game Series to the Cardinals; and then a rebuilt 1975 team lost a Game Seven to Cincinnati despite the legendary walk-off home run by Carlton Fisk that won Game Six.

Yawkey died in 1976, but the saga continued—good teams that just missed championships. Despite mismanagement by Yawkey's widow and estate (they lost the heart of their '75 team—Fisk, Fred Lynn, and Rick Burleson—to the effects of the new free agency system), they won another pennant in 1986 before dropping a fourth seven-game World Series, this time to the Mets; and this time, the Curse manifest itself in the sixth game when, with the Sox ahead and one out from victory and the title, a game-tying wild pitch was followed by a ground ball hit by Mookie Wilson that dribbled between first baseman Bill Buckner's injured legs, letting in the third and winning run of a bizarre inning.

Grady Little's managerial goof seventeen years later and Aaron Boone's homer completed a truly sorry run.

It was after the 1986 debacle that serious talk of the Curse of the Bambino began appearing, gaining broad acceptance in lore and rhetoric following publication in 1990 of a popular book by a wonderful writer, Dan Shaughnessy of *The Boston Globe*. People in what is self-admiringly called Red Sox Nation grasped the notion of the Curse like a drowning person desperate for a life preserver. The Curse allowed the Nation to ignore more obvious explanations for defeat, usually bad management that assembled weak teams.

And the tale of the Curse avoided the elephant in the Red Sox's room: race. As World War II neared its end, when it was clear that so many people of color had given so much to their country, the team was pressured along with most others to break the color line. In the face of considerable agitation from African-American writers and activists, as well as a prominent local politician, the Red Sox went through the motions in 1945 and arranged a three-player April "tryout" for three established Negro Leagues stars. One was Marvin Williams, a second baseman out of Philadelphia; another was outfielder Sam Jethroe, who would become the National League's Rookie of the Year with the more enlightened Boston Braves in 1950; and the third was Jackie Robinson, six months before Dodger president Branch Rickey made history with him in Brooklyn. After the "tryout," none heard a word from the Red Sox.

Tom Yawkey's insistence on a lily-white team was maintained through the fifties by two crony general managers, both Hall of Fame infielders—first Eddie Collins and then Joe Cronin. In the process, the Red Sox not only shamed themselves but also lost the talent wars handily. Few if any teams can pass on such talent and still succeed; certainly, the Sox could not. Yawkey eventually made it into the Hall of Fame himself, despite gaining infamy as the last owner to desegregate his baseball team, a full dozen years after Jackie Robinson debuted for the Dodgers.

This curse was said to have been lifted after all those decades when the team rebounded from the crushing loss to the Yankees in the 2003 playoffs to beat them in 2004 in what most fans (and all Sox fans) would say was the most thrilling comeback ever, all as prelude to sweeping the St. Louis Cardinals in the World Series. Lifelong fans who had for decades resigned themselves to defeat flooded Boston Common as well as downtown streets for a parade (the crowd estimate was in the millions). More than a few visited cemeteries to put flowers on the graves of deprived loved ones. And for good measure, the Sox won it all again three years later.

But the joy was followed by a return to accursedness in 2011, when in the span of a month the Sox fell from first place to a season-ending loss in the final game (baseball statisticians pegged their chance of missing the playoffs at just four-tenths of 1 percent with twenty-four games to play). Their free agent acquisition, Adrian Gonzalez, attributed the collapse to providence: "I'm a firm believer that God has a plan and it wasn't in His plan for us to move forward. . . . God didn't have it in the cards for us." But that was a minority view.

Talk of the Curse's return resumed in an orgy of criticism that resulted in the departure of the general manager, the dismissal of the manager, allegations of drinking and dissension among the players, and finger-pointing in almost every direction. For hopeful Brooklyn, the ecstasy of 1955 never dimmed. But for Boston, the defeat of 2011 had awakened the Curse with a force that made the joy of 2004 and 2007 fade.

The virulent atmosphere continued into the following season; several players got into public quarrels with the new Red Sox manager, Bobby Valentine. The team traded one of its mainstays, Kevin Youkilis, to the Chicago White Sox, and then as the severely disappointing season neared its end they unloaded three of their most expensive players (Gonzalez, Josh Beckett, and Carl Crawford) as part of a multiplayer deal with the Los Angeles Dodgers.

This nearly century-long story is a saga of triumph, outrage, ineptitude, struggle, rebuilding, lousy luck, and racism. But (in this Yankees fan's view of it) the real tragedy of the Curse, as it turns out, was not the Curse itself but Red Sox Nation's reaction to it. The real curse for Red Sox Nation was not failure to win the World Series but rather an incapacity to choose hope over despair—the embrace of a collective narrative of indomitable accursedness over the hopeful possibilities of waiting till next year. So thoroughly had the Nation adopted their despair that, during the dramatic 2011 slide, *The New York Times* reported a meeting of the Benevolent and Loyal Order of Honorable Ancient Red Sox Die Hard Sufferers (BLOHARDS for short) under the headline, AS SOX KEEP SINKING, TRUE FANS SUFFER WITH A SMILE.

There are exceptions to the general mood. In a beautiful eulogy of A. Bartlett Giamatti, the late baseball commissioner and noted Red Sox fan, Rabbi Robert Dobrusin showed a side of Red Sox Nation that signals there is hope of salvation for all humankind (in other words, even for Sox fans). The rabbi, writing in 1991, proclaimed:

> To be a Red Sox fan means to search for a way to understand how Fenway Park, with its green grass, close seats, hand-operated scoreboard, and all its history, cannot be allowed, *just once,* to fly a World Series championship banner. The championship would make Fenway Park perfect. Since 1918, however, that dream has gone unfulfilled.
>
> If all Red Sox fans suffer, an additional element of suffering comes from the perspective of the Jewish calendar. The Red Sox have a wonderful sense of timing. The greatest comeback in the team's history, in the fifth game of the 1986 American League Championship Series, happened during Kol Nidre. That same year, on Simchat Torah night, the Sox came within one strike of winning their first championship in sixty-eight years before collapsing. Our faith was tested by stretching to the limit the commandment to be happy on our festivals.
>
> It is the fate of Red Sox fans to be philosophical about the team.

In a letter to me, the good rabbi wrote, "Since 2004, my theology has changed quite a bit." I trust that for him at least the championship achieved that year brought the kind of permanently fulfilling blessedness that the 1955 championship brought for us in Brooklyn. Sadly, it did not for most of Red Sox Nation.

Hope and despair are two common though polar opposite responses to accursedness. A third possible response is acceptance—none of the high optimism of hope (let alone faith), yet none of the deep whine of despair. No team fills this bill like the Chicago Cubs.

The curse that afflicts the Cubs, like Boston's curse, has a history. The Cubs, like the Red Sox, were a dominant team in the early twentieth century—three consecutive pennants starting in 1906, including back-to-back World Series titles. And then, from 1908 to this day, nothing. No curse attended the World Series drought that ensued through World War II. The Cubs were a good, well-managed team, winners of three more pennants between 1909 and 1938. Some see a basis for this curse on the franchise in their last World Series appearance (1945). For those who accept this Genesis account, the curse persists despite the efforts of the man (Billy Sianis) who first leveled it, as well as his descendents, to remove it.

A Greek-American, Sianis had since the end of Prohibition run the famed Billy Goat Tavern (née the Lincoln Tavern) near the old Chicago Stadium, site of historic political conventions and hockey games. It was renamed after Sianis rescued a goat that had been injured falling from the back of a truck right in front of the place. Having nursed the animal back to health, Sianis named his watering hole after it, and the delightful if grubby Billy Goat became a regular stop for thirsty writers, politicians, and gangsters.

A flagrant promoter, Sianis showed up for Game Four of the 1945 World Series (the Cubs were leading, two games to one) against Detroit with two box-seat tickets and his goat, even parading the animal on the field before the game. Early in the game, however, the animal's odor proved so noxious that the front office demanded it be removed; when Sianis balked, he and the goat were unceremoniously paraded out of the ballpark. On the spot, all historical sources agree, Sianis leveled his curse: never another World Series for the Cubs. After they lost that October, he actually sent a sneering telegram to William Wrigley's surviving son and successor, P. K., wondering *Who smells now?*

Through the years, no organization has tried more earnestly to lift a curse than the Cubs. P. K. Wrigley publicly apologized to Sianis. A year before Billy died in 1970, he had himself removed the curse during the first serious postwar pennant drive by the team (however, superstitious fans believe the Curse of the Billy Goat may have been reinforced that year when a black cat cozied up to team captain Ron Santo while he was standing in the on-deck circle at New York's Shea Stadium near the end of the season). And Sianis's survivors have led several exorcisms over the years to no effect.

The truth is that even under P. K. Wrigley, the Cubs never achieved more than mediocrity for twenty-two years after the war ended. At one point, the team was so leaderless that they attempted on-field management by committee (the rotating group of eight was called the College of Coaches), with predictably disastrous results. But in the stands, the atmosphere rarely turned bitter. In fact, a ball game at Wrigley Field is as lovely a way to spend a day as exists in America; Wrigley really is a friendly confine.

The atmosphere has always been different in Chicago than in Boston. The one exception was the scorn heaped on poor Steve Bartman—the local businessman who with five outs separating the Cubs from the World Series in 2003 (just two days before the Red Sox succumbed to Aaron Boone's home run) prevented Cub outfielder Moises Alou from catching a foul ball, igniting a Florida Marlins rally that won them Game Six. Things got so bad for Bartman that Florida's governor at the time, Jeb Bush, actually offered him asylum.

Over the years, Cubs fans have accepted their fate with a measure of good cheer. For example, in the seventies, a group of transplanted Midwesterners (especially writers like George Will and the late David Broder) established in Washington, DC, the Emil Verban Society, named after a journeyman infielder who worked hard but compiled forgettable stats for the Cubs in the late forties. At an occasional lunch, they entertained themselves with trivia and stories, even importing an elderly Verban himself to meet President Ronald Reagan, also a society member. This jocular acceptance of unabated disappointment would have been unthinkable in hopeful Brooklyn or despairing Boston.

In truth, the Cubs' faithful fit nicely between the poles of Brooklyn and Boston, neither hopeful nor despairing; instead, they delight in their status as baseball's lovable losers. Tippy, for example, is a Cubs fan, though he has no connection to Chicago and has never been there. His reason: The Cubs frequently have led the National League in attendance, often in years when they have finished in last place. In his mind, they have earned his allegiance the hard way, even though his facts again are wrong.

But one suspects that the possibility of some magical day once captured in another place and time by those three simple words, *Wait'll next year,* lies somewhere in the heart of every Cubs fan—and that, if and when that day comes, its magic (like the magic that seized Brooklyn in 1955) will never die.

Adversity is baseball's handmaiden; coping with it is the game's great challenge—and its great lesson. As the writer Gay Talese put it in a *New Yorker* profile of Yankee manager Joe Girardi, "Like religion, the game of baseball is founded on aspirations rarely met. It generates far more failure than fulfillment." A player can lead one of the leagues in batting even though he gets a hit only once in three tries. The game's benchmark of great pitching, Cy Young, lost 316 times—more than anybody else who has ever thrown a baseball. Its most accomplished manager, Connie Mack, actually lost more than he won, doing so an astonishing 3,948 times. Errors are so much a part of the game that their total is on every scoreboard every day. The statisticians recorded the five-hundred-thousandth error in major league history (by short-stop Jose Reyes of the Miami Marlins) in 2012. For a team to finish in the middle of its pack, to win roughly as often as it loses, is usually to have a decent season no matter how high the ambitions of its players and the hopes of its fans in the defeat-free beauty of spring.

The Cubs' championship drought is a record; but others have also suffered. Indeed, there are several teams and towns that have had to cope with interminable adversity. In fact, twenty-three teams have had droughts of three decades or more, with two franchises (the Braves and the Pirates) doing it twice.

The Philadelphia Phillies held the distinction of playing their first ninety-seven years without a championship—a span lasting just shy of twenty presidential administrations—before they finally won it all in 1980. But Phillies fanatics, who've been described as many things (loyal, loud, intense, blue-collar, gruff, and downright rude), have never bought into the notion of a curse. They just chalked it up, loss after loss, year after year, to bad baseball.

Fans of other teams have done the same. A charter franchise of the American League, the original Milwaukee Brewers, went through sixty-five years and three cities before finally winning a Series as the Baltimore Orioles (most of their losses came when they were the St. Louis Browns).

And on the South Side of Chicago, the White Sox had a profound World Series drought of their own—one that lasted eighty-eight years, actually two years longer than the famous Red Sox curse. If baseball curses exist, perhaps the team that did the most to earn one would be the White Sox, whose best players accepted money from gangsters to intentionally lose the Series in 1919. Yet there never has been talk of a curse on the South Side. In all of these cases, a collective sense of cursedness just didn't crystallize, not for players nor management nor the greater community that rooted for the team. For these franchises and their fans, a championship is cause for joy, and defeat a cause for sorrow, but in the end it's about baseball—not curses (or the ecstatic moment of release called blessing). As with all hierophanies, baseball can be *a* catalyst to evoke the spiritual dimension, but it is not *the* catalyst for everyone, everywhere.

John Calvin, the sixteenth-century theologian who helped develop the second phase of the Protestant Reformation, wrote that on earth the state of mankind is completely depraved and sinful. To him, salvation came only through the unfathomable mercy of God and the gift of grace (to Calvin, the Yankees are "elected" and the Cubs are not). But maybe it all is much simpler. A shirt seen around Yankee Stadium during the Red Sox's free fall late in the 2011 season captured this thought. The front side reads with typical Bronx gusto, THERE WAS NO CURSE, and on the back, YOU JUST SUCKED FOR 86 YEARS!

Not to be outdone, an equally insightful shirt has been sold outside the friendly confines, which asks: WHAT DID JESUS SAY TO THE CUBS JUST BEFORE HE ASCENDED INTO HEAVEN? The answer: DON'T DO ANYTHING UNTIL I GET BACK. And another proclaims the words of the late, archetypal Chicago broadcaster Jack Brickhouse: HEY, ANYONE CAN HAVE A BAD CENTURY!

By now, the second century of World Series drought is upon them, but until it ends, Cubs fans will continue flocking to the corner of Clark and Addison Streets on game day—not because they expect to win, nor because they want to see how exactly they'll manage to lose, but simply because they want to be there. Just in case.

They sit, forever waiting to experience the ecstasy of release; the blessing that follows the curse. As Dougie and I did on October 4, 1955, when next year finally came. And today, it still feels just as holy as it did more than fifty years ago.

I t was the Fourth of July and the Cardinals, adorned in their traditional red and white, gathered to witness a special ceremony. But the setting was far from St. Louis, and the Cardinals were anything but ballplayers; they were the College of Cardinals, having convened at the Vatican for a ritual unlike any they had ever seen before. It was July 4, 993, the twentieth anniversary of the death of Bishop Ulrich of Augsburg, who in mere moments would be declared Saint Ulrich, in what is widely believed to be the first formal canonization by a pope.

In life, Bishop Ulrich is said to have been a wise, calm prelate who once mediated a rebellion against Otto the Great's growing empire, the one that would later be called Holy and Roman; he also organized the defense of Augsburg against invading Magyars. His pastoral cross was said to have healing powers, and villagers believed that women who drank from his chalice would have easy deliveries; in fact, he is still the patron saint of those facing difficult births.

It was in the two decades following Ulrich's death, however, that his name truly became associated with miracles. Many were said to have taken place at the exact site of his burial. So passionate became his following that houses of worship were named in his honor; many believed that merely invoking his likeness would generate an ability to heal (the barracks of the monastery that was built in honor of his sainthood remained intact for nearly a thousand years until destroyed in a battle during World War II). And a forged letter that emerged a full century after Saint Ulrich's death, written to support the right for priests to be married, was at first taken seriously simply because the signature on it was claimed to be his.

Saint Ulrich will never be confused with baseball's Ulrichs, George and Dutch, whose National League careers were so fleeting they would rank near that of the even less accomplished Archibald "Moonlight" Graham, made famous in the movie *Field of Dreams*. George played for twenty-three professional teams before retiring with a lone big league run batted in, while Dutch pitched sporadically over three seasons in the twenties, winning a grand total of nineteen games for the Phillies, baseball's worst team of that—and quite possibly any—time.

Venerating blessed persons is universal. Every religious tradition has its way of identifying and celebrating them, as do some secular ones. It should come as no surprise that the concept eventually reached baseball—and the shores of the lakefront town of Cooperstown, New York, where a museum was built to honor the legends (the saints) of the game.

From Christy Mathewson to Lou Gehrig, Damon Rutherford to Henry Wiggen, baseball's heroes—both factual and fictional—and the way we go about honoring and remembering them mirror the concept of sainthood that has been employed by religions over millennia.

The Jesuit theologian Pierre Teilhard de Chardin described the progressive spiritual evolution of humankind as a continually developing transformation culminating in a "supremely autonomous focus of union," what he called "Point Omega." For Teilhard, this evolution mirrors the stages of biological evolution, which he used as a metaphor: emergence (a new form), divergence (as the form propagates diverse forms), and convergence (a coming-together in a new unified form on a higher plane). Saints, in effect, are the foot soldiers of this process, displaying in their lives the limitless opportunities for spiritual development—in essence, an embodiment of the hierophanic experience. They are the best of what we can be.

In recent years, the Roman Church has made much of sainthood. Pope John Paul II, himself now beatified, canonized more saints than all of his predecessors combined, many of those he honored still unknown to even the most devout Catholics.

This sense of veneration is embedded within other religious traditions, even if the holy one goes by a name other than saint: prophet, miracle worker, or mahatma, to name a few. In the Abrahamic traditions, they serve dual roles as both role models and teachers.

Hebrew Scriptures identify no less than fifty-five prophets known as *Navi,* an abbreviation for a saying that translates to "fruit of the lips," emphasizing their anointed place as speakers for the divine. But the prophet is more than a spokesperson or foreteller. As Rabbi Abraham Joshua Heschel wrote, "Prophecy is the voice that God has lent to the silent agony, a voice to the plundered poor, to the profane riches of the world. It is a form of living, a crossing point of God and man. God is raging in the prophet's words."

The *Nevi'im,* the second of three major sections of the Hebrew Bible, is dedicated entirely to the prophets, covering a period of more than six centuries from the death of Moses to the Babylonian Exile. Selections are ritually read aloud in synagogue after the reading of the Torah on the

Sabbath and during Jewish festivals, a practice known as the haftarah. In them, prophets are repeatedly described as objects of persecution—in a sense, metaphors for the great struggles that have confronted the Israelites through history.

In Islam, miraculous acts have been attributed to the *Awliya,* in Arabic the "friends of Allah." They are celebrated today through festivals in their names and ceremonies at their tombs. Adam is considered to be the first prophet, and Muhammad the last, with all who came between them central figures of the Jewish and Christian narratives as well.

Together, the three traditions represent a pivot away from the polytheistic notion that saints are gods. Instead, sainthood serves to make concrete in a human being—a person with whom we other humans can relate—the power and effect of higher forces.

In Eastern religions, where often there is no separation between the spiritual and physical worlds, objects as well as humans can be spiritual beings. Readers of Bernard Malamud's celebrated novel *The Natural* may recognize this in the mystical powers of Roy Hobbs and his bat, Wonderboy, carved from timbers struck by lightning that is meant to evoke memories of Black Betsy, the venerated lumber swung by Shoeless Joe Jackson.

In the Eastern traditions, there are no formal processes to identify what Catholic tradition would call saints. Instead of being received from a higher authority, the special persons who are the equivalent of saints are gradually identified through what amounts to societal consensus. They are almost always noted for a deep commitment to teaching and to helping others. In the Hindu and Buddhist religions, it is often a person's internal development toward holiness that matters more than worldly activities. In Hinduism, there is the *swami,* a word derived from Sanskrit roots that literally means "an owner of one's self." Buddhist followers are taught to journey on the path to self-purification or *dhamma*. The attainment of *ariya*, referring to an especially noble-hearted person, is followed by personal striving to reach ever-higher levels of spirituality, four in all. In these faiths and virtually all others, however, individuals from the past are cited and studied for their inspirational value. *Saint* may be a Western word, but the essential concept is familiar everywhere.

Whatever the context and whatever its use, sainthood always has one salient characteristic at its core: a revelation of deep meaning. This is the hallmark of sainthood. Sainthood is the distinction bestowed for a life especially well lived; in effect, an induction into an honor society of those who are, as Teilhard might put it, the best of what we can be.

Baseball also celebrates its heroes. Each summer, the Hall of Fame induction ceremony in Cooperstown is filled with introductions that describe players as the "legends" and "immortals" of the game. A sense of timeless excellence pervades the Hall of Fame, from the Latin-style script (MVSEVM) chiseled above the redbrick entranceway to the gallery inside, lined with bronze-engraved plaques that honor baseball's most storied figures and personalities.

There is no greater debate among fans than over who deserves a place in the Hall. In any given ballpark on any given game day, a smattering of discussions in the stands inevitably turns to the chances of borderline candidates, like Fred McGriff; those who have been unfairly left out over the years, like Gil Hodges; and players who are as close to a sure thing as there can be, like Mariano Rivera.

Remarkably, the baseball writers who do the voting have never elected a player unanimously. Not Jackie Robinson, not "Hammerin'" Hank Aaron, not the "Say Hey Kid" Willie Mays, not the "Splendid Splinter" Ted Williams. Pitchers Tom Seaver and Nolan Ryan have come the closest, each garnering 98.8 percent of the vote. It is as much disgraceful as it is stunning that one in seven voters failed to cast a ballot for Sandy Koufax, the Dodger marvel who years later was named in a poll of two million fans as the greatest left-handed pitcher of the last century.

Two hundred miles to the south stands another baseball museum, this one just beyond the center field wall in Yankee Stadium. Monument Park has been aptly described by Brooklyn-born writer Allen Abel as a place "where plaques and standing stones honor the legacies of flyhawks, tycoons, and popes. (The numbers on the walls include 3, 4, 5, 7, 8, 9, II, VI, and XVI.)" At its center is a monument for the greatest Yankee of them all, Babe Ruth, which simply reads, A GREAT BALL PLAYER, A GREAT MAN, A GREAT AMERICAN. Ruth's life off the playing field often featured indulgent excess, but his central place in the game's lore shows how in baseball it is possible to be a saint on the field and a sinner in life.

This duality, a constant in all of secular life and not merely in baseball, is almost never a significant factor in religious stories, where such lines are by definition much brighter. In the Catholic Church, for example, where the concept of a saint corrupted by vice is as foreign as a virtuous demon, the mere publication of Mother Teresa's private struggles with her faith was jarring. Moments of human frailty in saints, like the denial and doubt exhibited by the apostles Peter and Thomas after the crucifixion, are fleeting.

In baseball, conflict and ambivalence often are inextricably part of the story. For starters, perspective is often central to how a fan feels about a ballplayer. Sal Maglie of the New York Giants was detested in Brooklyn until he became a Dodger and was loved; Mets fans loved Lenny Dykstra until he went to play for the Phillies; Minnesota fans adored their catcher, A. J. Pierzynski, until he took his much-publicized antics to the White Sox. And Yankees fans hated Johnny Damon when he played for the Red Sox (his two home runs in the seventh game of the 2004 American League Championship sank New York) but loved him after he joined the Yankees as a free agent; once he joined the Yankees, of course, the same Red Sox fans who earlier had adored him promptly despised him (after his departure, a prominent T-shirt in Boston included under a picture of the hirsute Damon the phrase LOOKS LIKE JESUS, ACTS LIKE JUDAS, THROWS LIKE MARY!).

Beyond such differences in perspective, however, there are players who, if judged only on their performance on the field, are true saints of the sport, but who simply are nasty persons at best, thugs at worst. Look no further than Tyrus Raymond Cobb.

Cobb was such a horrid person off the field that even in death his wild ride of a life—brilliant, thrilling, angry, bitter, vicious, and often violent—came back to complicate his legacy one last time. He was seventy-four when he succumbed during the summer of 1961 to cancer, prodigious amounts of whiskey, and far too many cigarettes. The month before he had entered Emory University Hospital in Atlanta with more than one million dollars in bonds from his portfolio in an envelope and, reportedly, a pistol.

At the funeral service in the north Georgia town of Cornelia, near the small village of Royston where he grew up, reporters estimated attendance at no more than 150 locals and relatives, many of them estranged. After his life of nearly three records-filled decades in baseball, only three former ballplayers and the executive director of the Hall of Fame bothered to attend the service. Two were catchers who had joined Cobb in Cooperstown: Ray Schalk, who pioneered the defensive aspects of the position; and Mickey Cochrane, who was briefly his teammate on the Philadelphia Athletics at the end of his career. The third was a fellow Georgian from the old days, a pitcher for the Brooklyn Dodgers named George "Nap" Rucker.

That was it. Before he died, Cobb told one of the few acquaintances who bothered to visit the hospital, the comedian Joe E. Brown, that he realized he was dying alone and that he was filled with regrets over a life he wished he had lived differently.

Cobb had first come to public notice while in the minors in Alabama through a short item in an Atlanta newspaper column by a budding sportswriter named Grantland Rice, who traveled to see Cobb play because he had received numerous postcards touting a young outfielder. Years later it was discovered that Cobb had written the postcards himself.

During his first year in the majors with the Detroit Tigers, when he was eighteen, Cobb's mother shot and killed his father. They had been married when his mom was twelve years old; she began having kids three years later (he was the first of three). His father, a local politician, suspected his wife of infidelity and so he sneaked up to their bedroom window trying to catch his wife unawares; alone that night, she mistook him for an intruder (or so she said) and blasted him with a shotgun. The following year she beat the murder charge at trial, but the weight of the killing and the doubts around it stayed with Cobb over the course of his career.

But what a career it was. After twenty-four years, he had amassed some ninety hitting records, sixteen of which were still standing when he died. Even today, his lifetime batting average of .367 seems safe, and only Pete Rose (and that's another sinner's story) has topped his famous hits total of 4,191. More than the records, however, Cobb was the high priest of the so-called deadball era in baseball, before the home run and Babe Ruth changed it all irrevocably, when the simple goal was to get on base somehow, advance, and then score.

Numbers don't quite tell the story of Cobb's dominance of one baseball category, the stolen base; vignettes do a better job. For example, the newspapers tell of at least four occasions when Cobb made it to first base and then stole second, third, and home. At least once, he tagged up and scored from third base on a pop-up, timing his dash home for the instant the infielder began his nonchalant toss back to the pitcher.

Nor do records do complete justice to his astonishing hitting skills. In 1925, toward the end of his playing career, Cobb told a newspaperman that for the next two games he was going to "swing for the fences" to prove his argument that hitting home runs was nothing special. He had nine hits and five homers. Indeed, during one season early in his career (1909) he actually won the American League's Triple Crown, leading in batting average, runs batted in, and even home runs (nine, every one of them inside-the-park, a league record). But that was also the third consecutive year in which Cobb had played a desultory World Series for his unsuccessful team (in those three Series he batted only .262); he never got another chance.

On a plaque outside of Detroit's Comerica Park, the Tigers' current home, Cobb is called a "genius in spikes." What it doesn't mention is that Cobb was notorious for using those same spikes, regularly and meticulously sharpened, as a weapon when sliding into a base. It was this vicious practice and his wretched treatment of teammates, opponents, and ordinary people that permanently stained Cobb's reputation; he snarled, he fought, and he attacked.

And his vile behavior permeated his life. He once slugged an African-American elevator operator and then stabbed the security guard who tried to intervene. During spring training in Georgia in 1907, he fought a groundskeeper and then choked the man's wife when she tried to stop his assault.

The most infamous incident occurred during the 1912 season against the New York Highlanders (now Yankees), when, after enduring a torrent of abuse from a heckler, he jumped into the stands the moment he heard the term "half nigger." As he pummeled the heckler, Cobb refused to stop hitting him after other fans yelled that the man had only one hand, famously snarling back, "I don't care if he got no feet."

For this behavior, the American League fined him fifty dollars and suspended him for ten days, prompting a brief sympathy strike by Cobb's entire team in a rare example of solidarity with him. Playing with young men recruited off street corners as replacements, the makeshift Tiger team lost 24–2 in Philadelphia behind the complete-game pitching of a fellow from St. Joseph's College who had never pitched a day in his life (he gave up twenty-nine hits and never pitched again).

Cobb often spoke bitterly of the chip on his shoulder, his most notable comment reeking of bitterness: "Sure I fought. I had to fight all my life just to survive. They were all against me. Tried every dirty trick to cut me down, but I beat the bastards and left them in the ditch."

The result was widespread unpopularity among players. Cobb's glaring absence among the group of mystical ballplayers that assembled at the *Field of Dreams* is explained succinctly in the film by Shoeless Joe: "None of us could stand the son of a bitch when we were alive, so we told him to stick it!"

An indifferent and occasionally violent parent and husband (twice), Cobb was in the end sorry after a fashion, but the toll on his bitter legacy could not be erased by occasional, near-death acts of generosity, made possible by the great riches he derived from his sizable investments. Shakespeare's Mark Antony said that "the evil men do lives after them; the good is oft interred with their bones." Or as Saint Paul put it in First Corinthians: "If I have a faith that can move mountains but have not love, I am nothing." By these measures, Cobb was a sinner. Still, Tyrus Raymond Cobb is enshrined in Cooperstown, a saint among baseball saints. And when judged for what he did "between the lines," he should be (I guess).

Though at a different position, Christy Mathewson, like

Cobb, was a dominating superstar on the field; off the field he was Cobb's polar opposite. When he died at forty-five in 1925 after nearly seven years of severe health problems flowing from injuries suffered in World War I, headlines cried: BASEBALL WORLD MOURNS and CHRISTY MATHEWSON IS DEAD. The word *idol* was used five times in the *New York Times* obituary, which declared him "the most consummate and brilliant artist of all time."

By the numbers, he was most likely the second best pitcher in an era of great pitchers early in the last century. His victories (373) were fewer than Walter Johnson's, as were his strikeouts (2,502) and shutouts (80). His New York Giants teams were better, winning five pennants compared with two for Johnson's Washington Senators; but what caused Hall of Fame manager Connie Mack to say he was better than Johnson was his command of games, especially big ones. Mathewson's career year was 1905. He won thirty-one games, had a remarkable 1.27 earned run average, threw eight shutouts including his second no-hitter, and struck out 206 batters. He then proceeded to win three games in the World Series against the Philadelphia Athletics—each a complete-game shutout, a feat not yet equaled.

And everybody loved him. Everybody. He had come from very little in the northeastern Pennsylvania village of Factoryville, named in the 1820s after a cotton mill took root there (the mill closed soon thereafter and there has never been another factory in Factoryville). Unusual for a ballplayer at the time, Mathewson was a college man. He attended Bucknell, where he was a football as well as baseball star and also his class president and a devout, observant Christian for good measure.

In *The Celebrant,* a terrific novel woven around the tale of this engaging, learned man, Eric Rolfe Greenberg wrote of Mathewson: "He was no less at ease in black tie than in his playing togs or the formal dress. . . . He did not so much fit into his surroundings as define them; he seemed innately, magnetically right in every circumstance."

In one scene, Mathewson conversed with ease about the rules that established baseball's foundation in the nineteenth century, balancing, as he put it, "the arithmetic of the game against its geometry."

"What a success he had! Don't you agree?" says Mathewson, speaking of the architect of baseball's rules. "All those balances—so exact, so demanding and tantalizing. Nothing in the game is easy, yet nothing is impossible. It's a game of intricate simplicity."

Baseball had not experienced anything quite like him in the new century. Most players were hard-living off the field. But Mathewson's refreshing wholesomeness gave the game new appeal at just the moment its sponsors had decided they wanted families, not rowdies, at their games.

Like Cobb, Mathewson answered his country's call the instant the United States entered World War I. Also like Cobb, he served in a special unit helping train soldiers for the new horrors of gas warfare (he was a captain). But during a training exercise in France, he was accidentally dosed with mustard gas, whereupon his health almost immediately deteriorated. He returned as a manager and executive, but tuberculosis eventually claimed him.

The day he died, October 7, 1925, was opening day for that year's World Series between the Pittsburgh Pirates and Walter Johnson's Senators. Baseball commissioner Kennesaw Mountain Landis decreed that every player would appear wearing a black armband, the first time that had happened. Even today, Bucknell plays its football in Mathewson Stadium, and the Saturday closest to his August birthday is still an official holiday in Factoryville. As it turned out, the good was not interred with his bones.

Mathewson, of course, was a huge celebrity in his day; on the strengths of his ability and character, he deserved to be. Interestingly, however, he was not the only player on those special New York Giants teams at the turn of the twentieth century about whom a novel has been written; indeed, he wasn't even the only pitcher.

Like *The Celebrant, Havana Heat* is both a tale of baseball and an allegory. It is a reminder of baseball's power to teach, inspire, and transport us. Darryl Brock's novel is built around the life and career of one of the handful of deaf people to make it in the major leagues. Luther Taylor was one of the mainstays on the Giants' pitching staff in those years. In the cruel vernacular of those days, he was called Dummy, to his face. He didn't care; if anything he was motivated by it. In less than a decade, he won 116 games before arm troubles slowed and eventually ended his career.

Brock's novel traces and imagines Taylor's remarkable life from a farm in Kansas to the fame and modest fortune of the big leagues to later fulfillment as a teacher and coach. But some of its most powerful and magical passages take place during a 1911 off-season trip the Giants made to Cuba. There, Taylor feels a spiritual tug—much more from the African-born religious world of Santeria than from conventional clerical forces. It is a specific call, directed toward a young Cuban pitcher, also deaf, whom Taylor mentors and who actually beats the Giants in an exhibition game; and it has broad implications, shaping the rest of his life.

As Allen E. Hye put it in his interpretive book *The Great God Baseball: Religion in Modern Baseball Fiction*, "The richness of [*Havana Heat*] lies in the many threads of Dummy Taylor's story that weave a bittersweet tapestry of life and draw us into the lives of people we grow to care about."

Among the threads is the 1905 World Series. Taylor was scheduled to start the third game. But rain postponed it; Mathewson pitched instead on the following day, threw the second of his three shutouts that Series, and Taylor never had another chance to play in the World Series. *Havana Heat* helps us understand why that doesn't matter ultimately. Mathewson's renown was national; but Taylor remains an iconic figure in the deaf community. The gymnasium at the Kansas School for the Deaf, where he was a long-ago valedictorian, was named in his honor shortly after he died in 1958.

Veneration is a universal phenomenon; but because it is done by human beings, the criteria, the process, and thus the decisions that elevate some to special reverence are varied and complicated. The record number of Catholic canonizations in recent years underscores the point, more a statement about the goals and methods of today's church than about the worthiness of human beings through history.

In worldly affairs, official veneration has evolved like so much of modern life into a series of processes with rules and, inevitably, bureaucracies, and therefore—again, because humans are involved—equally inevitable inconsistency and even hypocrisy. Today, there are halls of fame for scores of endeavors, from salesmen to craftsmen. The nation's first "Hall of Fame" was at my very own NYU, the Hall of Fame for Great Americans, begun in 1901, which after a vote taken at the 1900 World's Fair included among its first members George Washington, Ulysses S. Grant, Benjamin Franklin, and Samuel Morse (telegraph and code pioneer, NYU's first full professor, and painter). But the National Baseball Hall of Fame was the first for sports and it remains that rare combination of the specific and the generic.

Controversy has not surprisingly surrounded baseball's Hall of Fame almost from the initial selection of five magnificent ballplayers in 1936: Cobb, Ruth, Wagner, Mathewson, and Johnson. The arguments, however, have ranged far beyond accomplishment to character. Most of us want our heroes to be good people, but without ever saying so explicitly, the baseball establishment has ruled that criterion irrelevant. Ty Cobb was a wretched human being, but his volcanic, violent persona had no impact whatsoever on his enshrinement.

Within a decade, moreover, the Hall of Fame had welcomed two enormously significant figures—Cap Anson and Kennesaw Mountain Landis—who were key participants in the most damning black mark against baseball: the monstrous injustice of segregation, lasting from the professional game's infancy in the 1880s until Jackie Robinson and Branch Rickey (two baseball saints for sure) finally changed everything in 1947. Anson was one of the game's first superstars and used the power of his fame to agitate publicly for what came to be called the "color line" just after the professional leagues were formed. And no figure was more important in maintaining segregation than the commissioner of both major leagues himself, former federal judge Kennesaw Mountain Landis. But Anson was also one of the first truly great hitters, and Landis helped restore faith in the game's on-field integrity after the World Series of 1919 was fixed by gangsters.

Like many institutions, baseball tends to ignore moral dilemmas until forced to confront them, whether they be gambling at the dawn of the twentieth century or steroids at the dawn of the twenty-first. And like many institutions, baseball has offered a form of atonement, though not official acknowledgment of its failings: witness the veneration of Robinson today and the diligent efforts to mine the records of the old Negro Leagues to find stars (more than thirty so far) to anoint as Hall of Famers.

But there are limits to baseball's willingness to tolerate malfeasance; and two cases illustrate them. The first, very real, is the best known of the eight Chicago White Sox players banned for life due to the "Black Sox" scandal of 1919, Shoeless Joe Jackson (himself the title figure in a W. P. Kinsella novel that eventually became *Field of*

Dreams). The other is entirely fictitious, the complex Roy Hobbs, whom novelist Bernard Malamud christened *The Natural*.

Ty Cobb himself said Joe Jackson was the best hitter he ever saw and advocated his reinstatement. Babe Ruth said he based his own famous swing on Jackson's. After eleven amazing seasons, he was hitting .382 in 1920 when the final suspension happened; his lifetime batting average of .356 remains the third highest in baseball history. He was fast, fielded his outfield position magnificently, and had achieved hero status at the time he was suspended.

Jackson came from abject poverty, a sharecropping family in western South Carolina that was too busy surviving to permit any education whatsoever; but he was one of those special players in the early twentieth century who was beloved as well as admired, on a par with Wagner and Mathewson.

And then he lost it all. Sticking strictly to the uncontroverted facts about the scandal, the 1919 World Series was in fact fixed so that the extreme underdog Cincinnati Reds defeated Jackson's White Sox, five games to three. Something like one hundred thousand dollars changed hands, and Jackson kept five thousand of a promised twenty while staying silent about the shenanigans he knew were occurring. On the other hand, he never attended any meetings of the offending players and never agreed to do anything on the field during the Series. Quite the contrary, he was the Series hitting star, batting .375, getting a record-tying twelve hits, including a home run. Not a single one of the numerous questionable plays at bat or in the field was attributed to any action or inaction on his part.

The third highest batting average of the Series (.324) belonged to White Sox third baseman Buck Weaver, who also ended up getting banned from the game for life by Landis. Weaver never took a dime, played his heart out offensively and defensively, but was aware that a fix was in and also remained silent.

All eight players were acquitted of criminal charges associated with the scandal, but upon taking office Landis simply banned everybody and ignored appeals to reexamine the issue as the years passed. Jackson lived an honorable life as best he could. After a few stabs at semipro ball, he and his wife ran a dry-cleaning business in Savannah in the twenties and then a liquor store near where he grew up in Greenville until a heart attack claimed him in 1951.

In the law Landis once enforced, distinctions are critical to judgment, morally as well as legally. But in baseball, there are only "the best interests" of the game as viewed by one person alone. The power is arbitrary, which means it can be abused, sacrificing the very moral underpinnings of the judgments made. Joe Jackson was a fabulous ballplayer and by all accounts a fabulous person who made one, hideous moral blunder. Today he is often viewed as a victim rather than a perpetrator. From exile, Pete Rose understands baseball's need to keep the game free of gambling, but as one who claims he never let his compulsion affect his team's games, Rose would second the lament of Buck Weaver later in life: "There are murderers who serve a sentence and then get out. I got life." Joe Jackson could have said those words.

Baseball also is one of the best settings for metaphorical tales of the human spirit and character. If Shoeless Joe presents a complex case, then Malamud's character Roy Hobbs belongs to the philosophers. At nineteen, he is a star pitcher in the making, on his way by train for a tryout with (who else?) the Chicago Cubs. Among his fellow travelers is the Ruthian slugging champion Walter "the Whammer" Wambold, along with a mysterious, alluring woman, Harriet Bird—in fact a lunatic. During an impromptu stop at a carnival, Hobbs answers a dare, and from a makeshift mound strikes out the Whammer dramatically. In Chicago, though,

Hobbs impulsively answers a call from Harriet, goes to her hotel room, and is shot; she had originally targeted the Whammer but settles for Hobbs in her quest to remake the world by getting rid of arrogant athletes.

The novel resumes sixteen years later, with Hobbs a walk-on outfielder for the struggling New York Knights, led by a kindly veteran manager (Pop Fisher) and an evil owner (a judge named Banner) who is scheming to see his Knights lose the pennant so he can get rid of Fisher.

In his second try at baseball life, Hobbs encounters two women: Memo Paris, Fisher's femme fatale niece, who leads him on shamelessly; and Iris Lemon, a hardworking, wholesome woman.

Obsessed with Memo and needing money, Hobbs negotiates a thirty-five-thousand-dollar payoff from the judge to throw the Knights' final game. But Iris is there, and her presence inspires Hobbs to reverse course and make a last lunge toward greatness. With a chance to win, however, he is struck out by another young pitching sensation. Later that night, he punches out the judge and his bookie friend, dodges a real bullet from Memo, and throws the bribe money in her face. At the novel's end, he breaks down after seeing a late newspaper headline accusing him of throwing the game.

The novel, very different from the movie version starring Robert Redford, was at least partially inspired by a real event—the shooting of promising Phillie first baseman Eddie Waitkus in 1949 by a deranged young woman. Waitkus recovered from his chest wound and was baseball's comeback player of the year during the team's successful pennant drive (as the famous Whiz Kids) in 1950.

But Hollywood and real life aside, *The Natural* is a richly absorbing, tragic drama. The hero has deep flaws— ambition, lust, selfishness—that are nearly fatal. However, he also wrestles with his flaws, struggling to understand what matters and what does not. The themes are eternal.

The issue is not the Hall of Fame and baseball sainthood but the journey everyone takes toward whatever judgment awaits; along the way, most records, and not merely Shoeless Joe's and Roy Hobbs's, are mixed.

Because professional baseball is played by humans, it is hardly surprising that the sport reveals the human propensity to cut moral corners—and even to cheat. Some "cheating" in baseball—like stealing the other team's signs on the field—is seen as clever and not penalized. But breaking the rules of the game is more ambiguously accepted or rejected: stories of doctored baseballs and bats are legion. Players and teams undeniably try to bend or even get away with breaking the rules, but baseball seems prepared to tolerate the attempts as long as the violator accepts punishment if caught. More than one pitcher who got caught wetting or cutting a baseball has a plaque in the Hall of Fame. As the baseball cliché goes, it's "part of the game."

There is no written rule, but in its fitful, rarely courageous handling of human failings, official baseball has policed most carefully those offenses, above all gambling, that threaten the integrity of its product; by contrast, in recent years those responsible for the stewardship of the game have been lamentably late in addressing steroid abuse.

The story begins with the presence in the game of alcohol and substance abuse. For decades, liquor and baseball were practically synonymous, a fact of life that made clean livers (pun intended) like Christy Mathewson exceptions. Eventually, as understanding of substance abuse and its frequent companion, addiction, evolved, people with serious problems were treated differently, depending on how they handled their problem. Those lucky enough to get help or moderate their consumption were rewarded with affection; those who didn't were pitied more than hated, acquiring an aura of tragedy more than sin.

Fixing games, however, always has been the cardinal

sin. Even before Judge Kennesaw Mountain Landis arrived on the scene, baseball tried to be tough when players were caught betting or even associating with known gamblers, much less conspiring to fix games. Landis's hard line survives to this day, especially because Bart Giamatti gave it refreshingly moral force by his handling of the Pete Rose case. Rose remains banned; the only thing that has changed since 1989 is that he now admits his gambling that he once denied.

As steroids came into widespread use in the 1990s, official baseball was slow to answer a fundamental question: What exactly is the fan watching, a player who succeeds or fails through natural ability and hard work or a chemical marvel who is a function of his drug regimen? The judgment so far has been that performance-enhancing drugs (to use the official euphemism) strike at the game's integrity. It remains to be seen how, in the long run, the offenders of the steroid era will be treated. Will their records stand unblemished by asterisks? Will these offenders be eligible for the Hall of Fame? So far, the judgment appears to be severe: Barry Bonds, Mark McGwire, Sammy Sosa, and Rafael Palmeiro have suffered mighty blows to what would have been stellar reputations.

Judging others is a flawed endeavor, whether in the professions or athletics or even religion, because it is done by fallible humans. It is not for nothing that the Bible cautions in effect that what goes around comes around.

It was in this spirit that both flawed heroes, Joe Jackson and Roy Hobbs—quintessential sinner-saints of the baseball world—were confronted by a local boy who refuses to believe stories in the papers and asks his fallen idol to "Say it ain't so."

But it was.

It was a typically muggy summer afternoon in the nation's capital. The visiting, league-leading New York Yankees were thumping the cellar-dwelling Washington Senators as usual. The Yankees had just been retired in the top of the seventh inning on a harmless dribble in front of home plate by Gil McDougald, and were ahead 10–3. At that moment, just before Rocky Bridges of the Senators hit a triple to ignite a mini-rally, the youngest of the late President Gerald Ford's four children, Susan, was born—to her laboring mother's considerable relief.

On that day, July 6, 1957, Ford, then a Michigan congressman, had tickets to see the Senators at the old Griffith Stadium and planned on taking his young sons along. The onset of Betty Ford's labor changed all that, but at the hospital she couldn't help noticing that her husband, her sons, and even her doctor were distracted by the television images of the game as her labor intensified. Understandably displeased by their very divided attention, she made her feelings known as women in labor are wont to do. But not to worry.

"Susan was very cooperative," Betty Ford recalled years later. "She was born during the seventh-inning stretch, so we didn't disturb anybody." Whether the ordeal is a mother's labor or a tense ball game or a religious service, emotions and concentration are not infinitely sustainable.

Anyone who has ever been to a religious service is aware that the level of pious intensity occasionally abates; intensity must be relieved. All religious services therefore include what look (and sometimes feel) like intermissions.

Muslims, for example, are instructed about the when and where of the breaks in the sequence of their daily obligatory prayers.

Jews often separate afternoon and evening services (the *Mincha* and *Ma'ariv*) with a brief lesson (the *Shiur*) from an elder or rabbi that frequently discusses the sacred texts just recited in light of experiences in everyday life. In some Conservative congregations, as the Sabbath nears its completion, there is a longer pause to break bread, a chance not only to reflect but also to bond before continuing the prayers.

And Christians reserve time for choral or musical interludes that provide a few moments between rituals. From Christianity's earliest moments, there has been an imprecise division, imprecise but no less real, between the preparatory part of the service and the part where believers affirm their central faith or take communion or both. And in some liturgies, this transition is marked by the "kiss of peace" or the "holy kiss." Whatever it's called, it is another break in the worship, one that most definitely enhances the feeling of fellowship. But the atmosphere is different from the moments of communion with God. The kiss of peace serves, as do the musical interludes, as a pause—meaningful but different, a break in the intensity of the action.

Baseball fans get this. At the midpoint of every seventh

inning, we need no announcement, no request, much less a command. We simply rise from our seats. For some ninety years, this collective move has been accompanied by music—in most major league cases a very, very familiar song that dates to the early-twentieth-century days of Tin Pan Alley. The Wave may have come and gone, beach balls have bounced into distant memory, but the seventh-inning stretch lives on in every baseball congregation. Possibly the most famous pause in American culture, it is an occasion to salute the game. And it is a break in the intensity of the action.

This being baseball, the origin of the stretch is obscure and the subject of more than a little debate. The term cannot be found in print before 1920; the practice, however, appears to have started much earlier and to have begun because of the nature of seating in the game's early years. Many people simply stood for the entire game; those who sat occupied plain wooden benches—not the most comfortable resting place for the two or so hours a game consumed. It is not surprising that the folks on the benches would want to stand for a bit (and to avoid blocking views, that they would do it in unison and while there was a break in the action).

As far back as 1869, a letter from a pioneer of the professional game, Harry Wright (a British-born star ballplayer, later manager, and later executive with the original Cincinnati Red Stockings), described what certainly sounds like the seventh-inning stretch. As he wrote: "The spectators all arise between halves of the seventh inning, extend their legs and arms, and sometimes walk about. In so doing, they enjoy the relief afforded by relaxation from a long posture upon hard benches."

For his playing, innovation, and leadership, in both the development of the professional game and the formation of what became the National League, Wright is in the Hall of Fame—as is his accomplished brother, George, giving baseball its own Wright brothers twenty years before the aviation pioneers (also out of Ohio).

There is little evidence, however, of how widespread the practice of stretching was back then, much less when it became an established ritual. To fill out the picture, another story is worth a mention.

The man who brought baseball to Manhattan College in New York was Brother Jasper of Mary. He was not only the college's first baseball coach but also its prefect of discipline. Therefore, when on a muggy day in 1882 during the seventh inning of a tense game against a local semipro team, the Metropolitans, he called time and asked the student fans to stand and relax; they listened to him and stood in unison. It is said the New York Giants were so impressed by accounts of the event that they copied the stretch at their own games by the 1890s. Meanwhile at Manhattan College, the good brother is remembered well: The school's teams are to this day known as the Jaspers.

Even presidents got into the act. On Opening Day in 1910, William Howard Taft attended the game between the Senators and Athletics, his three-hundred-pound frame stuffed in a very small wooden chair down front. By the seventh inning, he was too uncomfortable to stay put, so he rose from his seat; nearly everyone else in the ballpark did, too.

Contrary to the claims of some, this is not the moment the stretch was born, but that day would become famous for another reason. Before the game started, the chief umpire handed Taft a baseball, which the President promptly threw to one of the players near home plate. Since then, every president has thrown out a first ball at least once.

Through the years, the details of the stretch have evolved; and it is not done uniformly across baseball. Various teams use different music to accompany the stretch. And one glorious tune has adorned it for decades. Riding the New York

City subway one day in 1908, the writer and vaudevillian Jack Norworth noticed a sign in the car: BASEBALL TODAY— POLO GROUNDS. Inspired, he began writing lyrics about a girl who is asked to a show but who has another idea, as she proclaims: "Take me out to the ball game." The music was written by another show business figure of the day, Albert Von Tilzer, who would have one more hit song, "I'll Be with You in Apple Blossom Time."

The baseball anthem was an instant hit, first sung by Norworth's very popular wife, Nora Bayes. The couple were everywhere in show business in 1908, together writing the smash hit "Shine On, Harvest Moon," which Bayes introduced. (A decade later Bayes also introduced and recorded George M. Cohan's World War I standard "Over There.") Neither Norworth nor Von Tilzer had ever been to a baseball game when their masterpiece debuted at the ballpark, and neither would see a game for decades. It hardly matters.

As time passed, "Take Me Out to the Ball Game" became more routine than special, until a new twist was added one day in 1976 on Chicago's South Side. It was then and there that the irreverent, most would say visionary, White Sox owner Bill Veeck Jr. persuaded a reluctant Harry Caray, then the broadcaster for White Sox games, to serenade the Comiskey Park crowd over the public address system.

As the story goes, much to the delight of fans who happened to be sitting nearby, Caray used to sing the song to himself while listening to the ballpark organist play it for the fans. Upon discovering this, Veeck proposed to Caray that he sing into a microphone so that all present could join him; but the broadcaster, who never fancied himself much of a singer, refused. Caray relented, however, once Veeck claimed to have recorded him in an earlier rendition and threatened to play it anyway. And baseball has never been the same.

When Caray moved across town to broadcast Cubs

games six years later and took his seventh-inning routine with him, the power of cable TV helped make the song special once again. Today, "Take Me Out" is one of the game's great fixtures, offered by choruses of players and fans at Little League diamonds and big league ballparks alike. At Wrigley Field, celebrities and politicians make the pilgrimage to Caray's old booth each game, often doing their best impression of the daffy broadcaster while they're there, to lead the friendly confines in song. On rare occasions, when a game goes deep into extra innings, those who stay are rewarded with the tune for a second time, since the Cubs are one of several teams that have made a tradition out of repeating the entire seventh-inning ritual midway through the fourteenth. For those dedicated fans, it is as Yogi Berra once put it, "like déjà vu all over again."

Many major league teams have put their own musical spin on the seventh-inning stretch by playing a hometown anthem immediately after "Take Me Out"—"Deep in the Heart of Texas" at Astros and Rangers games, the "Beer Barrel Polka" at Brewers games, and "Meet Me in St. Louis" at Cardinals games, to name a few. Baseball's other two birds, the Baltimore Orioles and Toronto Blue Jays, have created perhaps the two most unusual seventh-inning scenes in all the game.

In the seventies and early eighties, much of Baltimore fell under the spell of a maestro by the name of "Wild" Bill Hagy. Wild Bill didn't conduct an orchestra in the traditional sense (he actually drove an ice-cream truck or taxicab, depending on the season), but he created beautiful music nonetheless, leading thousands of fans in a nightly chant of O-R-I-O-L-E-S to start the stretch by contorting his ample limbs to spell each letter—a routine that became so popular it was even mimicked on television by Homer Simpson. All this from his perch in the upper deck and, later atop the home team's dugout at old Memorial Stadium. Around the same time as Wild Bill was joining the fray, another Oriole tradition began, this one continuing to this day. After singing "Take Me Out," the city crowd, inexplicably, joins in for a raucous singing of John Denver's "Thank God I'm a Country Boy," a practice that has since been copied by the more fittingly country Atlanta Braves.

In Toronto, the song "Take Me Out" was not at first part of the stretch ritual; instead, the club takes the seventh-inning stretch literally, as fans are led through a series of calisthenics exercises during the playing of a portion of "OK Blue Jays," a song that was once so popular in Canada its recording went gold. By contrast, when the expansion Florida Marlins introduced a similar exercise routine in 1993, those leading the drill were booed off the field almost immediately, never to return. But Toronto's status as the last major league team to do the stretch without playing Norworth and Von Tilzer's classic tune ended in the late nineties. Ever since, "Take Me Out" remains a staple in every park.

At Dodgers games, tradition dictates playing "Take Me Out" twice, with only the briefest of pauses in between. But not before "God Bless America" is played first.

Following the horror of 9/11, when baseball helped affirm a sense of community for a shaken nation, an executive from the San Diego Padres petitioned Commissioner Bud Selig to replace the jovial "Take Me Out" temporarily with the more patriotic "God Bless America." Selig, taken by the idea, instructed all thirty teams to do just that (although the idea of swapping songs soon morphed into just adding the patriotic hymn to what always had been done). And by doing so, baseball breathed new life into an American anthem that had fallen into disuse just about everywhere but the VFW hall and the old Spectrum in Philadelphia before hockey games.

Today, "God Bless America" is played at every game at Dodger Stadium in Los Angeles and Yankee Stadium in the Bronx. In 2001, just weeks after the tragedies in the city where the dust and smell of the destroyed World Trade Center still filled the air, the impact of "God Bless America" was palpable, deeply felt by every fan who came to Yankee Stadium. The national television audiences that watched postseason games that year also were stirred. More than a decade later, in New York, those feelings awaken each time fans rise for the stretch. The ritual has become less a break in the game than a service itself.

Other teams, among them the Nationals, Braves, Red Sox, and Mets, continue to play "God Bless America" on weekends and holidays as well as during the postseason, where it has become as accepted—and expected—as the pregame playing of the national anthem. Sometimes it's sung; sometimes it's played by organ, saxophone, or guitar; sometimes the crowd provides the chorus.

The seventh-inning stretch offers more than an occasion to get a beer, go to the restroom, or make a phone call. It offers time for reflection. For fans who experience the game in all its slow intensity, the pause heightens awareness, setting the stage for its culminating moments. The game, so wondrously slow while in motion, stands still.

The spark that will ignite the action again once the pause is complete has been present all along. During the break, baseball's second syllable either has been lying on the pitcher's mound or has been in the umpire's pocket. The ball, the game's sacred rock. Through the years its composition, design, and shape have been meticulously defined and only rarely changed. It is rubbed with a special mud and sometimes stored in humidors. Baseball's first syllable, the base, also receives special care, but the base never has achieved the special status of the ball.

The average ball is in play for no more than four pitches, and every game something like fifty of them wind up in a fan's eager hands, fair and foul, mostly to be kept and treasured. Some get signed by players; a few special ones get sent to the Hall of Fame to be kept in perpetuity. The stories and legends are legion, none better than my brother-in-law Mike Murray's (who, after a lifetime of inspired teaching in high school, now teaches my NYU class with me).

It was the summer of 1973. After nearly a quarter century of faithfully attending ball games, Mike was sitting in a general-admission seat in right field when his date asked him to get her a beer. Mike was headed toward a vendor when Bobby Murcer—the Yankee center fielder of the gloomy period—hit a shot off a Minnesota pitcher high into the evening air, headed straight toward him. What happened next so inspired him that he wrote an op-ed piece about the thrilling experience that *The New York Times* published.

"Within seconds, a twenty-three-year odyssey, fraught with Sisyphean disappointment and Stygian gloom, came to an end," wrote Mike, then thirty-one. "I was experiencing Nirvana. My life had come full circle. . . . Now, as autumn and winter approach, and I am confronted with the bewildering prospect of huddles, red dogs, game plans, the bomb, and the blitz, I can take solace in the white orb enthroned on my coffee table. When piercing gusts rattle windows and the whole world is gulping down martinis, scotch sours and the turbid, martial cant of football, I will curl up on the couch under a quilt, the ball ensconced safely in my hands, and dream the dreams of my youth."

Mike's piece caught the eye of the commissioner of baseball, who quickly sent in tribute and gratitude another baseball—this one signed by all the living participants of the first All-Star Game in 1933. On my sixtieth birthday, in an act of extraordinary love and generosity, Mike gave me both baseballs.

Stories of the ball abound. One collector, Seth Swirsky, used to own *both* the ball that went between Bill Buckner's legs, costing the Red Sox Game Six of the 1986 World Series (Swirsky also owns a bottle of the champagne that on that fateful day was on ice in anticipation of the celebration that never occurred) *and* the ball that famously hit outfielder Jose Canseco on the head, bouncing past his outstretched glove into the stands for a home run.

Even more bizarre is the story of a pair of game balls from a 2012 contest between the Atlanta Braves and the hometown Cincinnati Reds. Perfectly located in a left field seat, Reds fan Caleb Lloyd caught two home run balls hit in consecutive at-bats, only three pitches apart. The first he kept himself; indeed, since he knew it was Mike Leake's first major league homer (Leake is a pitcher), he prevailed upon Leake to autograph it after the game. The second, a homer by Cincinnati shortstop Zack Cozart, he gave to the friend who had gotten the tickets for the game and who actually worked hard to convince Lloyd to attend. The Reds made Lloyd an honorary captain for the next day's game and, as he took out the lineup card before the game, identified him on the scoreboard as a "professional home run ball catcher."

But nothing was quite like the scene one day in 1957 in Philadelphia's Connie Mack Stadium, captured more than a half century later by journalist Bob Levin in the (Toronto) *Globe and Mail*: "Sometimes the trivial runs transcendent, in a moment so improbable that it endures as a metaphor for the vagaries of life. . . . The perp was the Phillies' Richie Ashburn, a future Hall of Famer who slashed a foul [ball] into the stands that hit a fan, one Alice Roth, smack in the face, bloodying and busting her nose. Play was halted as medics worked on her (her eight-year-old grandson, trying to fetch the offending ball, was told by the man who'd nabbed it, 'Go to hell, kid'), then resumed as she was laid on a stretcher. On the next pitch, Ashburn slammed another foul—cracking Roth on the knee as she was carted out. What are the odds? Ashburn visited Roth in the hospital and they became friends, forever connected by the cruel whims of the baseball gods."

And then there is Leonard Kriegel's story of his youth as a Bronx boy felled by polio during World War II, a particularly poignant account of a baseball's sacred power. While languishing upstate in a rehabilitation hospital, his legs useless, his uncle Moe—seated in the Yankee Stadium bleachers one day in 1945—engaged a group of pitchers in the first-place Detroit Tigers' bullpen about his disabled nephew's condition. Moe extracted a promise: If the Tigers won the pennant, they would send a ball, autographed by the entire team, to the hospital. They did, on both counts.

Kriegel credits that gift with prompting the first stirrings of the imagination that led him to a writing life. For him, "that ball simply embodied the idea of physical grace—a grace that had been ripped from my life by the virus."

The ball and his relationship to it carried him through the travails of a polio-afflicted childhood to maturity in his love both for baseball and for life. Kriegel held on to his ball, treasured it even, but in time came to feel that it was feeding not only his imagination but also his illusions about the world his condition prevented him from fully joining. One day, leaning against a parked car across the street from his building, Kriegel was playing catch with a friend when the ancient ball they were using simply fell apart. Remembering his autographed baseball, he told his friend to fetch it and, then, they put it in play—and in peril.

"One by one, the names on the ball disappeared, chalked and cut and scuffed into oblivion by granite and brick and creosote. That baseball, autographed by the entire Detroit Tigers team on the day they clinched the pennant in 1945, would never again feed my illusions. For one last time, it had rescued me from a bad day"—connecting him to something greater. So it has been for many over time.

And so it is for us. Our liturgical stretch complete, the ball, sacred symbol and reality, remains in play for us as well, and so the game continues.

For Damon Runyon, one of the most celebrated scribes ever to cover a baseball beat, the postgame hangout wasn't far away, less than ten miles from all three New York City ballparks. The name of the place was Lindy's.

With his days chronicling the Giants daily now behind him after World War I, for the first time in years Runyon was able to watch games just for fun. And with no story to file, if traffic was light he could make it from his box seat to his booth in the restaurant in less than half an hour.

On any given night in the Roaring Twenties, Lindy's hosted a dizzying mix of newspapermen, actors, and gamblers, each group staking a claim to its own section of the place, the cheesecake mecca of Manhattan. Legend holds that the famous recipe was held under lock and key, even decades after namesake Leo Lindermann had died and the delicatessen had closed its doors for good.

Sometimes Runyon would venture across the room to hear the latest from his old pal, Arnold Rothstein. To the untrained eye, Rothstein looked pretty much like the other customers—average height and build, hair carefully parted an inch or so from the center in the style of the time. He was impeccably dressed, usually in a perfectly knotted bow tie and a stylish three-piece, pin-striped suit (the kind that couldn't be found on the racks at Wanamaker's), the uniform of most of the men among the after-theater congregants. Rothstein simply was part of the scenery. He was there night after night—eating, drinking (always milk), cavorting, scheming, and above all taking and placing bets. Rothstein spent so much time at Lindy's that after a while he started to call it "the office."

Almost everybody who entered the office had at some point heard the sensational story of how the World Series back in 1919 was fixed, with no less than eight Chicago players on the take or in the know. But few realized that the man sitting at the corner table—his back to the wall—holding court with the likes of Runyon and scores of other baseball fans, was the one who is believed to have actually done the fixing.

F. Scott Fitzgerald based Meyer Wolfsheim, a character in his masterpiece, *The Great Gatsby*, on Rothstein. After being introduced to him, the novel's protagonist, Nick Carraway, reflects, "It never occurred to me that one man could start to play with the faith of fifty million people."

Nearly a century after the scandal, baseball remains America's faith—a civil religion. The game's capacity to thrill, inspire, and galvanize the masses is undeniable.

The term *American civil religion* was coined by sociologist Robert Bellah in the sixties. He used it to describe shared beliefs, symbols, values, and rituals, independent of—or parallel to—the explicitly religious traditions. As Bellah put it: "Although matters of personal religious belief, worship, and association are considered to be strictly private affairs, there are, at the same time, certain common elements of religious orientation that the great majority of Americans share. These have played a crucial role in the development of American institutions and still provide a religious dimension for the whole fabric of American life."

For the better part of two centuries, the national pastime has been an important thread in that fabric. From makeshift games on city streets to the grandeur of the major leagues, baseball is one of the enduring symbols of Americana, so much so that a popular General Motors jingle made the claim:

They go together in the good ole USA,
Baseball, hot dogs, apple pie, and Chevrolet.

But if baseball is a secular institution that sometimes displays the elements of the classic religions, it is not just because it attracts committed (even fanatic) fans as religions attract ardent believers or because it builds ballparks as religions erect cathedrals. It is that baseball has the capacity to elevate and transform, that it has a power to bring people together in expanding levels of relationship: parent and child, neighbor and friend, community and city, state and the nation. On some majestic summer days, the many who assemble are one.

Arguably the most beloved three hundred words ever spoken in a baseball park came from Lou Gehrig as the Yankee legend told a hushed, reverent stadium crowd on July 4, 1939, that he was leaving baseball to battle the condition that would kill him two years later. Scholars of rhetoric still study his simple address for its power, eloquence, and thematic unity as he spoke of the "bad break" that did not shake his conviction that he was "the luckiest man on the face of the earth." The packed stadium was church-quiet while this strong, stoic man spoke. The interruptions were not cheers but rolling rounds of applause—one lasted two full minutes. His words affected each person who heard them individually; and they stitched the crowd together in a wonderful, unified tapestry.

In their book *All Things Shining*, Hubert Dreyfus and Sean Dorrance Kelly wrote of the Gehrig story and how that moment and moments like it galvanize communities, uniting them in a sense that there is something beyond.

"The sense that one is joined with one's fellow human beings in the celebration of something great reinforces the sense that what one is celebrating really is great," they wrote. "Moments like this take on greater meaning when they are shared with a community of like-minded folks who are experiencing the same kind of awe. Whether it is in the church or in the baseball stadium, the awesomeness of the moment is reinforced when it is felt as shared by others. When it is also shared *that it is shared*—when you all recognize together that you are sharing in the celebration of this great thing—then the awesomeness of the moment itself bursts forth and shines."

Even if baseball was not invented by Abner Doubleday in an upstate New York cow pasture in 1839 (a claim first made in 1907 but later convincingly refuted), the Cooperstown creation myth reveals how baseball reflects the American ethos: Doubleday, after all, was a major general in the Union army and a hero during the Civil War.

"[Baseball] is to games what the *Federalist Papers* are to books: orderly, reasoned, judiciously balanced, incorporating segments of violence and collision in a larger plan of rationality, absolutely dependent on an interiorization of public rules," wrote Michael Novak in *The Joy of Sports*. "Baseball is designed like a federal system of checks and balances." It is no coincidence that for years the American and National League logos have been varying blends of bald eagles, stars, and stripes.

At the root of American civil religion, Bellah explained, is the notion of American exceptionalism, not exactly the slogan shouted by politicians, but the real thing: "Behind the civil religion at every point lie biblical archetypes: Exodus, Chosen People, Promised Land, New Jerusalem, and Sacrificial Death and Rebirth. But it is also genuinely American and genuinely new. It has its own prophets and its own martyrs, its own sacred events and sacred places, its own solemn rituals and symbols. It is concerned that America be a society as perfectly in accord with the will of God as men can make it, and a light to all nations."

By the late 1880s, baseball's popularity across different social classes was embedding it in the DNA of the America Bellah described. As Mark Twain said at the time, "Baseball is the very symbol, the outward and visible expression of the drive, and push, and rush, and struggle of the raging, tearing, booming 19th century!" Christopher Evans, coeditor of *The Faith of 50 Million,* wrote of the early game: "In the eyes of its prognosticators, the game balanced rugged manliness and athletic acumen with social acceptability."

At the turn of the century, immigrant communities began to notice the central place of baseball in American life, embracing the message that was stated clearly half a century later by French historian Jacques Barzun, "Whoever wants to know the heart and mind of America had better learn baseball, the rules and realities of the game." This view of America endures. Just four years ago, a young Korean woman in my NYU class explained that she had taken the course "because the two most important things to understand about America are baseball and religion."

Abe Cahan, as the editor of *The Jewish Daily Forward,* recognized that what was quickly becoming the national game could be a vehicle for assimilation; so he began, in editorials as early as 1903, to urge his readers—largely first-generation immigrants from Europe—to allow their boys to play baseball. "Let us not so raise the children to grow up foreigners in their own birthplace," he wrote pointedly. Indeed, for Americans baseball became a birth-right; more than a few fathers have described placing gloves inside their child's crib in infancy (and at least one of those glove-toting toddlers, Curt Schilling, grew up to be the Most Valuable Player of the World Series).

Ethnic groups started gravitating toward stars who were of and from their community, ranging from "The Flying Dutchman" Honus Wagner ("Dutchman" as in Deutsch, since his heritage was actually German) and "Germany" Joe Schultz to "Bocci" Ernie Lombardi. Nearly a dozen big league ballplayers have been nicknamed "Irish." But in the days before Jackie Robinson changed everything, no single ballplayer represented as much to a single segment of the population as Hall of Famer Hank Greenberg did to Jewish Americans.

With Greenberg's Detroit Tigers competing for their first pennant in a quarter century in 1934 and the High Holy Days fast approaching, the first baseman was forced to make a choice. Greenberg was so anguished by the decision that he sought the advice of a rabbi, who through a creative interpretation of biblical text justified—even encouraged—his playing on Rosh Hashanah, the Jewish New Year. And so he did just that, hitting two home runs in a 2–1 victory over the Boston Red Sox and, in the process, helping the Tigers to extend their lead to four and a half games. They clinched the pennant twelve days later.

Henry Ford, a notorious anti-Semite, probably gasped when he picked up the next morning's *Detroit Free Press* to see bold Hebrew script staring back at him; "Happy New Year" it exclaimed in translation. A few days later, as the regular season was ending, Greenberg decided not to play on Yom Kippur, his religion's day of repentance and most solemn time of the year, and instead went to synagogue to pray. He received a standing ovation the moment he walked into the sanctuary. Greenberg's decision foreshadowed a nearly identical one three decades later, when Dodgers ace pitcher Sandy Koufax sat out the first game of the World Series against the Minnesota Twins on Yom Kippur, giving a new generation of Jewish baseball fans another hero.

An ode to Greenberg appeared in the newspaper on Yom Kippur, written by Edgar A. Guest, who would later become Michigan's first—and to date only—poet laureate. It ended with a flourish:

> We shall miss him on the infield and shall miss him
> at the bat,
> But he's true to his religion—and I honour him for
> that!

While the Tigers were winning the '34 pennant, philosopher John Dewey was giving a series of lectures at Yale, which later gained widespread distribution in published form as *A Common Faith*. In them, he justified faith as something dynamic and evolving in an age of social and scientific progress, describing the essence of religious experience as too full of awe to be captured in doctrine. "Ours is the responsibility of conserving, transmitting, rectifying, and expanding the heritage of values we have received that those who come after us may receive it more solid and secure," Dewey concluded. "Here are all the elements for a religious faith that shall not be confined to sect, class, or race. Such a faith has always been implicitly the common faith of mankind."

The traditions and elements of baseball fit nicely with Dewey's idea. From its huge fan population to its collection of rituals to its tall tales and homespun charm, the game's lore is carefully passed down and then built upon, from one generation to the next. And while pockets of fans may choose to root solely for one of their own, the joys of experiencing baseball often extend much farther, its common faith accessible to anyone who simply revels in the beauty and gifts of the game.

Baseball had become so ingrained in the national consciousness by World War II that President Franklin Delano Roosevelt wrote what became known in baseball circles as the "Green Light Letter" to Commissioner Kennesaw Mountain Landis less than six weeks after the bombing of Pearl Harbor: "I honestly feel that it would be best for the country to keep baseball going. . . . Here is another way of looking at it—if 300 teams use 5,000 or 6,000 players, these players are a definite recreational asset to at least 20,000,000 of the fellow citizens—and that in my judgment is thoroughly worthwhile."

Shortly after Roosevelt wrote his letter, the St. Louis Cardinals started sending a baseball cap to pilots of the US Marines' famous Black Sheep Squadron for every Japanese aircraft they shot down. A photograph of twenty aviators wearing Cards caps continues to hang today in the Smithsonian National Air and Space Museum, just steps from the Capitol. And baseball sent more than caps. Many ballplayers, including stars like Greenberg, Boston's Ted Williams, and Cleveland's Bob Feller answered the call to duty (much as Christy Mathewson and others did during World War I). The national pastime became intertwined with national service.

Today, ironically as a result in part of the presence in Japan of General MacArthur's troops after World War II, America is not the only nation with a passion for baseball. Japan's love affair with Seattle Mariner (and later a Yankee) Ichiro Suzuki, who set a record by collecting more than two hundred hits in each of his first ten major league seasons, runs so deep that millions of people oceans away stay up through the latest hours of the night and the earliest hours of the morning to watch him play on television. In this regard, they are imitating thousands of Roberto Clemente fans in his native Puerto Rico and throughout Latin America who followed his every move over the course of a storied career.

So revered was Clemente, who died in a plane crash in 1972 while attempting to deliver aide to earthquake victims in Nicaragua, that statues, bridges, public schools, parks, and stadiums have been named in his honor in no less than three countries. He is one of only a few players for whom the Hall of Fame has waived its usual five-year waiting period before candidacy (he was voted in on the first ballot). "The mythic aspects of baseball usually draw on clichés of the innocent past," Clemente's biographer David Maraniss wrote. "But Clemente's myth arcs the other way, to the future, not the past, to what people hope they can become. His memory is kept alive as a symbol of action and passion, not of reflection and longing. He broke racial and language barriers and achieved greatness and died a hero."

At its most potent, the unifying power of baseball is in the passion that builds in communities over its 162-game season, often leading to huge downtown rallies and parades of the kind usually reserved for presidents, war heroes, and astronauts.

Randy Johnson was no stranger to such adulation; yet he had one day that was special for its generosity of spirit. Nearing the end of his amazing pitching career, Johnson had the good fortune in 2009 to find himself in baseball's moral center, St. Louis. He had already passed the milestone few pitchers have ever reached—three hundred victories—and was earning his last paychecks working for the San Francisco Giants. This day, he was pitching against the home team Cardinals.

Lifted in the late innings just before the All-Star break, and clearly on his way to pick up victory number 303 (which turned out to be the last in a twenty-two-year career), Johnson was startled to see the entire crowd at the new Busch Stadium rise as one to cheer him, a kind of thanks-for-the-memories ovation to a worthy opponent from what is arguably the most closely knit, tradition-soaked baseball community in the country. On this day, the rabid St. Louis fan base expanded their community by one—no matter that he was wearing the other team's uniform.

Johnson may have been startled, but he was not surprised. The middle-American river town has enjoyed a revered reputation for generations among baseball wags. As Johnson himself has put it, "It's a fun city to come to because you know it's all baseball."

And baseball there is played famously hard and well, from the spikes-high "Gashouse Gang" rowdies of the thirties to the mad dashes on the base paths of Enos "Country" Slaughter in the forties, to the elegance of Stan "the Man" Musial in the fifties, to the glare of fiery concentration on the face of the Hall of Fame fireball pitcher Bob Gibson in the sixties. Though the record must show that this border-state city was notoriously hostile to Jackie Robinson during his rookie year, the St. Louis tradition generally has been that the game is left on the field, that opponents are respected, that booing is for Easterners, and that rooting for the home team is no less intense during lean years.

St. Louis may just barely be among the twenty largest metropolitan areas in the country, but in recent decades only the far larger-market Los Angeles Dodgers and New York Yankees have kept pace in attendance. When the Cardinals drew three million fans for the first time in 1987, only the Dodgers had done it. Their success was magnified by a famous radio station, KMOX, one of the first fifty-thousand-watt behemoths on the scene; in the years before the major leagues expanded, KMOX saturated the South; if you lived in Dixie, you were a Cardinals fan.

Much of baseball's enormous, lasting attraction flows from its ability to stitch people together, to create communities, to foster bonds of lasting power based on shared memories and experiences. It doesn't happen everywhere and it doesn't happen all the time, but when it does it is extraordinary to behold. An unusually large national television audience got more than a sniff of this in 2011, when the Cardinals awoke from ten and a half games behind the pack in late August, salvaged playoff eligibility on the last night of the regular season, and upset what were on paper two much better teams (Philadelphia and Milwaukee) to get to the World Series. Once in the Series, they beat the heavily favored Texas Rangers in seven games, including a Game Six come-from-behind victory in extra innings that ranks among the most thrilling baseball games ever played. In two separate, potentially terminal innings, the Cardinals were down to their very last strike. Their victory unleashed an ecstasy worthy of Beethoven, incapable of expression in words alone. An entire rejoicing community rose mightily to proclaim its joy.

Baseball's communities exist in a web of expanding concentric circles, from the nuclear to the national. Nothing is deeper than the bonds we share with parents and loved ones. And for many, such bonds were nurtured by what some people call "a catch" and others insist is "a game of catch." One of baseball's delightful arguments is a question of syntax: Do two people play catch or have a catch? Whatever the right words to describe it are, they describe an intimate pastime, for many emotionally associated with childhood or parenthood or (as in my case) both. The ball goes back and forth hypnotically, as life outside the arc slowly fades away and only the ball and the partner remain; sometimes there is conversation, often no words are required. Just quiet intimacy interrupted only by the pop of ball colliding with leather.

The final scene of *Field of Dreams*, Phil Alden Robinson's adaptation of W. P. Kinsella's novel *Shoeless Joe* (as in Jackson), is, of course, a game of catch. Ray Kinsella has built the ball field in his Iowa cornfield, the eight players banned after taking Rothstein's money in 1919 have reappeared to play against a pickup squad of old-timers, and a bitter and reclusive writer has had his idealism rekindled enough to join the story. As the old-timers walk off the field into the tall corn one last time, one player, the catcher, hangs back. The catcher is Ray's father, not yet into the life of disappointment and semi-estrangement we know he will lead; in this moment, he has been transported back in time to a place where he can be happy playing the game he loves. He is a modest talent still dreaming.

Ray introduces the young catcher to his wife and daughter; it would be unthinkable to destroy the moment by telling John Kinsella what the future holds for him and them. As he begins to walk away again, Ray calls out suddenly, "Hey, Dad, you wanna have a catch?" "I'd like that," his father-to-be says.

The ritual tossing continues as the camera pans to show the line of headlights stretching to the horizon, cars bringing people to the Iowa ball field (more than two decades after the movie's release, thousands of ordinary folks still come to that cornfield, drawn by the magic). In this scene, the tiny circles of parent, child, and family merge with a larger community of those who let baseball's delights bring them together. The meaning of the moment had been foreshadowed by the writer character (J. D. Salinger in the novel, a fictional Terrence Mann in the film to avoid trouble from the reclusive and litigious real-life author):

I don't have to tell you that the one constant through all the years has been baseball. America has been erased like a blackboard, only to be rebuilt and then erased again. But baseball has marked time while America has rolled by like a procession of steamrollers. It is the same game that Moonlight Graham played in 1905. It is a living part of history, like calico dresses, stone crockery, and threshing crews eating at outdoor tables. It continually reminds us of what once was, like an Indian-head penny in a handful of new coins.

Like a congregation in a house of worship, the members of baseball's ultimate community, the outermost circle, share that faith. It lives now in the hearts of thirty major league towns and countless others. For me and my circle, it thrived as never before or since in Brooklyn; and for me, my unconflicted son, and thousands of others, it continues today with the very different New York Yankees.

There is a cliché about life in Brooklyn while the Dodgers were there: You could walk down one of the borough's broad boulevards and follow a Dodgers game on the radios blaring through the open windows of apartments and storefronts. It might be myth (the Truth-carrying kind that sometimes is not factual) that you could follow every pitch, but it is beyond doubt that as you walked one of the borough's two dozen neighborhoods, you easily could keep track of a game through the lilting erudition of Red Barber and then the harder consonants of young Vin Scully (horror of horrors, he was actually from the Bronx).

The Brooklyn community was suffused with the Dodgers' achievements and failures between 1941 and their departure for Los Angeles; and it delighted in seven National League pennants. The ingredients of this community were there for all to see and feel: the affection for the team's core of approachable stars, almost all of whom lived in one of the neighborhoods; the pride that it was their huge, diverse borough that was home to Jackie Robinson's courageous breakthrough; and the collective defiance of despair and cynicism that saw them through six World Series defeats at the hands of the Yankees and the loss of three pennants on the final day of the season.

And all of this was cemented by the power of radio, a blizzard of broadcasting that filled the airwaves not only of New York but also of the entire country. Amidst it all, there was one voice that is not so well-known today but was certainly known to a huge audience back then that belonged to a man named Nat Allbright. Allbright was not a New Yorker (indeed, as far as can be determined, he never saw the Dodgers play except in spring training), but in the fifties he was the voice of an unprecedented network of stations (more than one hundred) that broadcast simultaneous re-creations of Dodgers games. From a studio near Washington, DC, where he spent his long career (he died in 2011), Allbright mastered the art of giving pitch-by-pitch reports from snippets of wire service transmissions, complete with a variety of recorded crowd noises and tricks like a tap of a pencil eraser on his microphone to mimic the sound of bat meeting ball. The listeners knew, of course, that this was an imaginative enlivening of wire service data; and for the millions that made it even more special.

A young Ronald Reagan got his start doing Cubs games this way out of Des Moines in the thirties, before moving on to his career in show business and eventually finding work in an Oval Office not far from Allbright's broadcast booth. But relatively few fans heard Reagan, the broadcaster. Allbright's audience, by contrast, was enormous—for two important reasons that reveal the concentric circles of baseball community.

One was simply Brooklyn's enormity: It was the fourth-largest city in the country at the time of its reluctant annexation to the rest of New York at the end of the nineteenth century (and it would be the fourth-largest city today if it ever broke away from the rest of New York). Moreover, because throughout American history, Brooklyn has been both a destination for immigrants and a gateway to the rest of the country for their children, its national ties are especially large; experts in demography have calculated that one of six (maybe more) Americans either lived there or has a close relative or ancestor who did. And consciousness of roots has always been a defining feature of this Brooklyn diaspora.

The second reason was race, always a punctuation mark for important American stories. In the years before teams used chartered jets to move around the country, they usually arrived by train late in the evening before a road game. In the late forties and fifties, the Dodgers frequently disembarked in some town to be met, no matter what the hour, by crowds—mostly African-American fathers with their young sons in tow who sought, in respectful silence, a glimpse of Jackie Robinson.

Nat Allbright's Dodger network was therefore no accident. The Dodgers were America's team back then. And in a virtuous circle, he both profited from that fact and helped build it. In 1955, the year Brooklyn finally won it all, the team gave him a World Series ring.

The Yankee dynasty that beer baron and owner Colonel Jake Ruppert constructed in the twenties with general manager Ed Barrow had become after World War II something more like the Roman Empire (many a Yankee foe compared them to US Steel, and Red Sox president Larry Lucchino famously dubbed them "the Evil Empire").

But in spite of (perhaps because of) their success, best symbolized by their five consecutive World Series victories (1949–53), the Yankees were not America's team; indeed, outside their natural fan base, they more often faced antipathy

("Damn Yankees" was as much a national cry as a popular musical).

Here, too, the story was, at least partly, about race. It was not until the 1955 season that the Yankees introduced their first African-American (outfielder-catcher-first-baseman Elston Howard, who would make the final out in the Game Seven loss to the Dodgers that autumn), and it was not until after the owners sold the team nearly a decade later that the Yankees became truly color-blind. We want our heroes to be good as well as great, though we often manage to turn a blind eye to their vices. Somehow, however, between Joe DiMaggio's record-shattering hitting streak of fifty-six games in 1941 and the pursuit by Roger Maris and Mickey Mantle of Babe Ruth's home run record twenty years later, genuine affection for the Yankees was difficult to find.

That began to change in the late seventies, driven as much by the tribulations of New York City as by the return of Yankee success. In this period, beginning my second decade as a reborn Yankees fan, I was living in Washington and clerking for Chief Justice of the United States Warren Burger. One of the many rewards of the year was a lunch with each of the Supreme Court justices. When my time came with Justice William Brennan, it was not long after the Yankees won it all in both 1977 and 1978. Justice Brennan, an avid fan who did not abandon the Dodgers when they moved west, turned the conversation at lunch to baseball.

I noted how all of New York had been caught up in the Yankees' reemergence. After the city's near-bankruptcy, its long and painful road back to solvency, and its horrid problems with crime and neighborhood decay—as flames engulfed the South Bronx during Game Two of the '77 Series, ABC broadcaster Howard Cosell famously told the nation, "There it is, ladies and gentlemen, the Bronx is burning"— the Yankees provided a spark of hope, something to cheer.

Justice Brennan, though a New Jersey product, had

been in his youth, like me, a passionate Brooklyn Dodgers fan. He said he disagreed about the newfound appeal of the Yankees, summing his views up with a single word, uttered with contempt that was rare for him: "Steinbrenner." As in George III, the Ohio- and then Florida-based shipbuilding magnate. The synonyms and phrases evoked by that surname summarize the force of Brennan's argument—self-ensnared in Watergate money crimes, free-agent-era poster child, managerial musical chairs, leader and bully, rule-stretcher and -breaker, two suspensions from active management of his franchise, legitimate celebrity and shameless headline hound, control freak, dramatic victories and maddening defeats.

The justice had a point. The return to success—based in large part on the Yankees outspending teams to bring in free agents like Reggie Jackson—had a tinge about it that stood in the way of the kinds of communities that grew up around teams like the Cardinals and Dodgers. But I had a point, too. It mattered greatly to New York that it have a winner—and to far more people than those who simply rooted for the Yankees. New York was supposed to be a preeminent city, and for the first time since what seemed like forever (of course, it had been only a decade since the Mets' Miracle Year), they had a baseball team big enough to match the city's own ambitions.

The evolution of the Yankees and their role in both New York and the national community reached critical mass after 1996, thanks in large measure to a single, quiet man of enormous character—not Steinbrenner, but a guy from Brooklyn, whose St. Francis Prep baseball teams battled my own alma mater, Brooklyn Prep. Joe Torre, from the moment his team came storming back from a two-game deficit to take the 1996 World Series from the favored Atlanta Braves, gave the country powerful reasons to like the Yankees—reasons beyond simple success. His inner strength wordlessly communicated to Steinbrenner: "Lay off." And Steinbrenner largely did.

A combination of Torre's skill at the game he had once played magnificently and his quiet humility allowed a new generation of largely homegrown ballplayers to share his spotlight (this would change somewhat in later years with the acquisitions of superstars such as Jason Giambi, Roger Clemens, and Alex Rodriguez). The team that the city and the country came to celebrate was built around homegrown talent: Derek Jeter, Bernie Williams, Jorge Posada, Mariano Rivera; lunch-pail players like Tino Martinez and Paul O'Neill joined them, bringing their own formidable skills; and there were contributing-role players who would have their moments in history, like Scott Brosius and Aaron Boone.

The bulk of the regeneration was accomplished before the horror of 9/11. After the attacks, the Yankees helped unite a more than stricken town; they gave the country more than an entertaining distraction. For a change, it was not championship baseball that drew attention, it was really, really good baseball played by people you could admire at a time of intense national grief. In baseball terms, it was in many ways the ninth-inning and extra-inning heroics of the team in the 2001 World Series against Arizona that inspired—even after the ninth-inning defeat in Game Seven deflated the hopes of a championship. In a sense, the Series demonstrated the continuing power of baseball to bring people together for something more than merely baseball.

The evocative, unifying power of the game runs from the sandlot to the corridors of power in America, and even to the Supreme Court. So it was that in a 1972 opinion for the Court involving a challenge (by former St. Louis Cardinal star Curt Flood) to the clause in baseball's standard contract stifling players' mobility, Justice Harry Blackmun could not resist waxing poetic on the central position of the game in American culture—thereby revealing a love for baseball I later witnessed firsthand over our late-night chats during the year I worked at the Court for his fellow Minnesotan, Chief Justice Burger (the two jurists, both appointed by Richard Nixon, were called by many "the Minnesota Twins").

Justice Blackmun eagerly cited a passage from the lower court opinion: "Baseball's status in the life of the nation is so pervasive that it would not stain credulity to say the Court can take judicial notice that baseball is everyone's business. To put it mildly and with restraint, it would be unfortunate indeed if a fine sport and profession, which brings surcease from daily travail and an escape from the ordinary to most inhabitants of this land, were to suffer in the least because of undue concentration by any one or any group on commercial and profit considerations. The game is on higher ground; it behooves everyone to keep it there."

Then, in the midst of his own account of the history of the game, Justice Blackmun took a detour, the fan bursting from within, and offered his list of nearly ninety of the game's most legendary figures. In the best tradition of baseball's "hot stove league" (the debates that rage among fans over the winter), Blackmun said he offered his list to provide "tinder for recaptured thrills, for reminiscence and comparison, and for conversation and anticipation in-season and off-season."

The list has attracted attention ever since. It includes many of the obvious greats: Ty Cobb, Babe Ruth, Walter Johnson, and Christy Mathewson. But it also includes Hall of Famers known to a smaller circle of hard-core fans: Wee Willie Keeler, Carl Hubbell, Rube Marquard, George Sisler, and Eppa Rixey (most wins ever by a National League left-hander until Warren Spahn supplanted him).

The good justice's list also displayed his command of

trivia: Deacon Phillippe, who started the very first modern World Series game in 1903 for the Pirates, beating Cy Young of the Boston Americans; Germany Schaefer (three guesses where his parents were from), who amazingly pioneered the art of stealing first base (with runners on first and third, he would steal second, hoping to attract a throw that would enable the runner on third to score; then if the catcher didn't throw to second, he would dash back to first on the next pitch and try again, a ploy that led to a rule banning the running of bases backward); and Charlie "Old Hoss" Radbourn, one of the first nineteenth century pitchers to make the Hall of Fame, a three-hundred-game winner who in 1884 won fifty-nine or sixty games (depending on which version of history you prefer) in nearly seven-hundred innings of work—records not likely to be matched ever again—and whose leg injury is often said to be the origin of the term *charley horse*. Finally, there are Harry and Stan Coveleski, pitcher brothers from the teens and twenties. Harry is pure trivia but Stan is in the Hall of Fame, not only for his 215 victories but also because he was one of seventeen pitchers permitted to continue throwing the spitball after it was banned in 1920; two other spitballers also are honored who won even more than he did (Burleigh Grimes and Urban "Red" Faber).

Justice Blackmun also offered a nod to the talent brought to the major leagues when the color line broke. So he included Jackie Robinson and Branch Rickey as well as Satchel Paige and Roy Campanella. However, just as many of the Court's opinions leave observers guessing, so also Justice Blackmun's list contains a glaring ambiguity: he listed Sad Sam Jones, but he does not make clear whether he meant the solid American League pitcher (229 wins between 1914 and 1935) or the pitcher from the fifties and sixties who was the first African-American to hurl a no-hitter.

In the end, the justice's opinion, as he predicted, served only to start arguments, not end them. It undeniably is, however, an illustration of the power of baseball and its function as an element of our civil religion.

It is that extra dimension that defines religious communities as something more than congregations that gather for services. As Jesus said in the Gospel of Matthew, "When two or three are gathered together in my name," a greater spirit also is present.

So also where baseball communities large and small convene—from father and son playing catch to a nation turning its collective eyes to Yankee Stadium after 9/11— wherever they gather, a spirit lives that reveals a dimension beyond what appears to eyes and mind.

The crowd at Fenway Park turned its collective attention to the man standing atop the dugout. They watched as he meticulously adjusted his bowler hat and tie, took a deep breath, and lifted the oversize, pylon-shaped megaphone toward his mouth. With as much force as could be mustered, he cried into it, introducing the home team players, each of whom was greeted with raucous applause.

Stomping and shouting, the fans watched their guys take the field wearing the traditional home team uniforms, all white, interrupted only by black belts and, of course, the bright red stockings stretching to the knee that gave the team its colorful name.

Mere minutes later, same ballpark, same crowd but a different scene entirely: The sun had dipped below the stands and out of sight, bringing the illuminated signs that pitched beer, sneakers, and insurance companies sharply into view. Booming speakers blasted rock and roll while high-definition images filled the giant screen above center field. The iconic Green Monster in left sprang to life with the latest scoring updates from far-flung ball fields—one had Florida hosting Tampa Bay. Fans could be spotted eating that modern ballpark staple, sushi.

It was "Throwback Night," a journey from baseball's present to its past and back again. The game, played less than two months into the 2011 season, commemorated the Chicago Cubs' first visit to Fenway in nearly ninety-three years, when they played the final games of the 1918 World Series that the Red Sox won—a contest made famous by Babe Ruth's dominant pitching, and kept famous by the ensuing curse that eventually took his name. A sense of novelty permeated the 2011 game. However, the great irony was that the fans most interested in baseball tradition were those most likely to be offended by the matchup; this was, after all, interleague play.

The following season, the Red Sox–Cubs game was trumped by an even more elaborate celebration honoring Fenway Park's hundredth anniversary. More than two hundred former players and coaches were present—most poignantly the wheelchair-bound, excellent infielders of the forties, Bobby Doerr and Johnny Pesky (who died that summer). From the stands you could see the two best-known foul poles in the game: the one in left field that Carlton Fisk hit in the 1975 World Series and the one in right field that is named after Pesky, who hit a famous home run to the short porch that it marks. In left field stands The Monster, as evocative as ever.

The Dodgers, even in Los Angeles, brought every living member of the Brooklyn team that won in 1955 back for a perfect weekend fifty years later. And for more than sixty years, the Yankees have invoked Jeter's "ghosts" at Old-Timers' Days that have drawn all their great ones, from Babe Ruth through Joe DiMaggio and Mickey Mantle, to Ron Guidry. Baseball fans savor the emotion of such days and have never resisted the chance to see a hero one more time, even when the setting is scarcely the same and the players' skills have long since yielded to age.

Nostalgia is one of baseball's defining attributes. The game's past shadows its present—always there to be conjured for instruction, to prod memories, and to revive dormant emotions. Nostalgia is the tribute the present pays to the past.

The quaint, throwback uniforms that the Red Sox and Cubs revived for their modern fans to enjoy were different from the originals in one important respect: the numbers stitched to their backs. In the early twentieth century, uniforms didn't identify players. The first short-lived experiment with numbers involved the Cleveland Indians in 1916; there was another fleeting attempt by the Cardinals in 1923; but it took the mighty Yankees in 1929 to inaugurate a custom that quickly spread through the majors, becoming a requirement for teams on the road by the early thirties. But the Yankees never added names to the numbers: to this day, the Yankees, unlike all other teams, have only numbers on their home and away uniforms.

At first, New York used the numbers to identify players according to their batting order (hence, Babe Ruth with number 3 and Lou Gehrig with 4), but the practice of assigning them less logically quickly took hold. Once players had fixed numbers, it became possible to memorialize a great player by retiring his number for all time on that team (or in the unique case of Jackie Robinson decades later, on all teams).

It is largely lost to history that tragedy started it all. The first retired number, in fact, was Gehrig's on the Yankees, following his courageous revelation that he was suffering from the disease that killed him. Babe Ruth's was retired in 1948, when he was dying of cancer.

Uniquely, there is Cincinnati's number 5. It once belonged to one Willard Hershberger, a decent catcher and the backup to Hall of Famer Ernie Lombardi on the Reds' winning teams just before World War II. Hershberger is the only major leaguer to have committed suicide during a season. A victim of depression, he slit his throat in a Boston hotel room in the summer of 1940. The Reds immediately retired his number (or at least did not reassign it) and dedicated the rest of their season to him. After they won the World Series, Hershberger's teammates voted him a share of their proceeds, giving the money to his grieving mother. During the war, however, the Reds revived the number, thereby making it available a generation later for a promising young catcher named Johnny Bench.

Since then, more than one hundred and fifty ballplayers have had their numbers retired by the major league teams for which they played. In every case save one, they were established stars in—or with a plausible claim to be in—the Hall of Fame. And every ballpark has some kind of display to celebrate its team's special numbers (some have grandiose names like Ring of Honor or Level of Excellence). The exception: Pittsburgh's number 1. It belonged to Billy Meyer, who knocked around the minor leagues, and occasionally the majors, before being named Pittsburgh's manager at a horrible time in their history. In 1952, Meyer's team won 42 and lost 112 games, the worst record for a Pirates team ever. The manager, however, was both popular and hardworking, and two years later (by then he was a team scout) his number was retired in tribute to baseball's Job.

For the serious fan, old uniforms and numbers are to be venerated and treated with respect. To his dismay, a marvelous southpaw named David Wells (himself a huge fan of baseball tradition) was reminded of this in 1997. A standout pitcher in the free agent era who eventually won more than two hundred games (one of them perfect), Wells was in his first year with the Yankees when he took to the mound one day, wearing a hat he recently had purchased, one that Babe Ruth had worn in 1934. Wells was a Ruth fanatic, living by a larger-than-life credo that evoked memories of the Babe and wearing the number 33 (the closest he could get to Ruth's retired number 3) on his back. In retirement, Wells even got a tattoo depicting himself pitching to the Bambino, naturally on his left arm. He wore Ruth's antique hat for all of one inning before manager Joe Torre ordered him to remove it and fined him. The official reason: a breach of league rules (they call them uniforms for a reason). But to a traditionalist like Torre, wearing Babe Ruth's hat was sacrilege. Wells, who had paid thirty-five thousand dollars to buy the hat, later sold it at auction. Throwback games, retired numbers, and the Wells episode illustrate how deeply we long for the past—not necessarily the past as it was; quite often, in fact, a romanticized version of it (the way that the Old West wasn't actually the Wild West of John Wayne, with six-shooters and swinging saloon doors).

As the author Stanley Cohen put it: "Baseball, almost alone among our sports, traffics unashamedly and gloriously in nostalgia, for only baseball understands time and treats it with respect. The history of other sports seems to begin anew with each generation, but baseball, that wondrous myth of twentieth century America, gets passed on like an inheritance."

Passed on and cherished; phrases like *The Boys of Summer* touch a warm, deep place, indescribable (ineffable) in its evocative power.

Nostalgia permeates religious tradition as well. Mircea Eliade wrote that the "nostalgia for origins is equivalent to a *religious* nostalgia. Man desires to recover the active presence of the gods; he also desires to live in the world as it came from the Creator's hands, fresh, pure, and strong." This journey home (also baseball's ultimate goal) is what Eliade called the *myth of eternal return;* an experience that goes beyond merely marking an event to *reliving* it.

For religious man, the experience is traditionally evoked by ceremony (liturgy), often centered on food and drink. For Roman Catholics, the miracle of the Eucharist is transubstantiation: The "substance" of the bread and wine becomes the "substance" of the body and blood of Christ at the moment of consecration, even as the "accidents" (the appearance) of bread and wine remain. By doctrine, in the mass, the Last Supper and Christ's sacrifice on the cross is made present, its memory is celebrated, and its saving power is applied. We return *in illo tempore* (to the special, sacred moment), transported existentially to another plane. The Last Supper, of course, was a Passover Seder, a focal point of the Hebrew calendar, itself rich in a ritual retelling—and reliving—of the story of the Israelites' exodus from Egypt, in part through the elements of food on the Seder plate. As Eliade put it: "Through the reactualization of his myths, religious man attempts to approach the gods and to participate in *being*."

Eliade's extensive study of religion shows us how nostalgic ritual goes beyond memorializing sacred events to rekindle the powerful reality and experience embedded within the sacred myth, and by doing so provides a powerful bridge to the transcendent plane that was touched in the earlier time.

In this spirit, novelist W. P. Kinsella depicted a mystical journey through time to shortly after the turn of the twentieth century, where his characters discover—what else?— the last Chicago Cubs team to have won the World Series, playing an epochal game against a local team.

The journey of the main character, Gideon Clarke, actually begins when his father, Matthew, confronts a blinding flash of lightning (shades of Saul on the road to Damascus) while he and Gideon's mother share their first kiss. The bolt imprints in Matthew's memory all the box scores of the Iowa Baseball Confederacy and the story of a visit paid by the Cubs to play an exhibition doubleheader on July 4, 1908. The site of the game was an Iowa hamlet originally known as Big Inning (as in the biblical "in the *beginning* was the Word"), later as Onamata. The Cubs' opponent was an All-Star team from the Iowa league.

But there was a problem with what Gideon's dad knew. The Cubs' front office flatly denied the existence of the July 4 game, the Iowa Baseball Confederacy, and even the town; and there was no discoverable evidence that the game or the league ever existed. Matthew was certain he knew the truth, and he set out to prove he was correct. His certainty became an obsession, and the subject of his graduate school thesis (he wanted it to be in history, but university officials insisted it should be in fiction writing). His life ends in despair at a Milwaukee Braves game when he leans headfirst into a vicious line drive hit toward him in the stands. In that instant, his knowledge of the game and the league (and his obsession with both) are transmitted to his son, Gideon, who takes up his father's quixotic cause.

The most important twist in the story occurs when Gideon and his friend Stan Rogalski, armed with a revelation from a dying neighbor who had participated in the game, go to a section of a railroad track outside their town known as the Baseball Spur. There, they pass through space (and the intersection Eliade called *axis mundi*) and time to Big Inning, arriving at the 1908 game itself, which is played in a continual, torrential rainstorm. The two apparently mismatched teams play a maddeningly close game and, because it is baseball, there is no clock. The first game of the doubleheader lasts a biblical forty days, through 2,614 delightfully tortuous innings. No second game was played.

As they mine the past, not just pine for it, Gideon, Stan, and others resolve some of their real-life issues. Stan had always hoped for a shot at the majors; he plays in the game, acquits himself well, and gets an offer from the Cubs. Gideon has an unsatisfactory marriage; but in his 1908 world he finds a local girl, Sarah Swan, with whom he shares true love until, in a cruel twist of fate, she is killed in a car accident during a delay in the game.

Kinsella's magical storytelling provides a wonderful metaphor. The Iowa All-Stars' right fielder is a statue, the Black Angel of Death, who snares fly balls in her wings. The game is secretly manipulated by an ancient Native American, three hundred years old, who believes his late wife's reincarnation is impossible unless the Iowa team wins (in the end, he engineers this result by hitting the game-winning home run).

As the game proceeds, the Cubs' bosses in Chicago try to halt it, aware that their regular season is in jeopardy; but the players refuse to stop. No less than Teddy Roosevelt suddenly appears and enters the game for Iowa, only to strike out. A huge balloon descends from the sky, occupied by none other than Leonardo da Vinci himself, who plausibly claims to have both invented baseball and designed the enchanting symmetry of the ball field. "Unfortunately," he laments, "I lived in a nation of bocce players," and by the time baseball became popular his connection to it had been lost to history.

Above all, the hero of the novel is baseball itself. Gideon Clarke explains:

> "Why not baseball?" my father would say. "Name me a more perfect game! Name me a game with more possibilities for magic, wizardry, voodoo, hoodoo, enchantment, obsession, possession. There's always time for daydreaming, time to create your own illusions at the ballpark. I bet there isn't a magician anywhere who doesn't love baseball. Take the layout. No mere mortal could have dreamed up the

dimensions of a baseball field. No man could be that perfect. . . .

"And the field runs to infinity," he would shout, gesturing wildly. "You ever think of that, Gid? There's no limit to how far a man might possibly hit a ball, and there's no limit to how far a fleet out-fielder might run to retrieve it. The foul lines run on forever, forever diverging. There's no place in America that's not part of a major league ball field."

As if to prove this point, one Confederation outfielder, William Stiff, chased a fly ball from Iowa all the way to New Mexico, his feet slashed by cacti and yucca plants.

Inevitably, *The Iowa Baseball Confederacy* contains its share of interesting characters drawn from the annals of actual baseball history—for example, Cubs Hall of Fame pitcher Three Finger Brown (he actually had four fingers). Brown lost virtually all of the index finger on his pitching hand to a farm accident, but because his middle finger had been mangled in a fall and was essentially worthless to him, he had only three that worked. His real name was Mordecai Peter Centennial (he was born in 1876) Brown; he won 239 games, and his career earned run average of 2.06 is still the lowest ever for a pitcher who won more than 200 times (edging out Christy Mathewson). Imagine the discipline it took Brown to relearn how to throw a baseball, to generate enormous topspin from his unique grip, with the stub of his index finger against the ball. As a reward, his unique curve-ball broke down and away from right-handed hitters, pro-ducing thousands of harmless ground balls over the years.

When Gideon and Stan return to their real lives, they are the better for their nostalgic journey. They have experi-enced existential return (the first assignment in my seminar asks students to offer a theory of connection between works by Eliade and Kinsella's *Iowa Baseball Confederacy*.)

Kinsella's tale is fantasy, of course. But occasionally baseball literally mixes past and present—quite palpably in those powerful moments when an aging veteran puts an exclamation point on a great career by coming alive one last time. Baseball's saints remain revered even in decline (witness the respect shown to Lou Gehrig and Babe Ruth and to Bernie Williams and Jorge Posada in New York as their once towering hitting numbers faded).

So thousands were thrilled when Ted Williams in 1960 hit his 521st and final home run in his very last at-bat as a major leaguer. At forty-two, and a veteran of two wars, his final season was one marvelously long good-bye—a home run on Opening Day, plus twenty-eight more that same year. The last scene was captured perfectly in the words of John Updike, who in an essay about that day in *The New Yorker* depicted a different Tao from what he had described four years earlier from his perch in the Yankee Stadium bleachers:

> Though we thumped, wept, and chanted "We want Ted" for minutes after he hid in the dugout, he did not come back. Our noise for some seconds passed beyond excitement into a kind of immense open anguish, a wailing, a cry to be saved. But immortality is nontransferable. The papers said that the other players, and even the umpires on the field, begged him to come out and acknowledge us in some way, but he never had and did not now. Gods do not answer letters.

And even today, many remember the day that Grover Cleveland Alexander, almost at the end of a twenty-year career that produced more pitching victories than all but two other players, walked slowly to the mound in Yankee Stadium as a thirty-nine-year-old Cardinal. It was the bottom of the seventh inning of Game Seven in the 1926 World Series. St. Louis was ahead, 3–2, but the Yankees loaded the bases with Hall-of-Famers-to-be Earle Combs, Ruth, and Gehrig; there were two outs, and a genuine clutch hitter, Tony Lazzeri, was at bat. Old Pete, as Alexander was known, had endured the horrors of combat in World War I and had battled booze in his great career, but he had one more grand performance in him, striking out Lazzeri and pitching hitless balls the rest of the way to preserve the Cardinals' victory. Hollywood was of course watching, too, and Ronald Reagan would eventually play Old Pete in the movies.

And then there was the day in 1984 when another thirty-nine-year-old, Tom Seaver, his glory years with the Mets behind him, was summoned by a young White Sox manager, Tony La Russa, for his first relief appearance in eight years because the team had no options left. It was the twenty-fifth inning of a 6–6 game against Milwaukee, and La Russa had run out of pitchers. Seaver would have to pitch, despite the fact that he was scheduled to start the very next game. Had he lost, it would have been his thirtieth loss in just over two years, double his number of victories.

But he won. He retired the Brewers in order, including their slugger, Robin Yount, just before Harold Baines hit a home run to win the marathon game for Chicago. That evening, Seaver went out and pitched eight and one-third innings in yet another White Sox win.

In his next start, he pitched a complete game.

And in his start after that, he did it again.

For two wonderful weeks, the baseball world lit up as Seaver reminded everyone how good he once had been. Those who witnessed this magnificent "return" experienced ineffable joy beyond expression. Heads shook in wonder and wide smiles filled faces. No words would do; none were needed.

But words—some words, at least—were needed as postscript to the metaphysically thrilling Game Six of the 2011 World Series between the Texas Rangers and the St. Louis Cardinals. David Freese's home run cleared the center field fence to give the Cardinals a come-from-behind-twice victory and force a Game Seven (which they won). As the ball settled on a grassy knoll behind the fence, broadcaster Joe Buck simply said: "We will see you tomorrow night."

Buck's line was virtually the same as one that had been spoken spontaneously on the air twenty years and one day before—by his late father. It was another Game Six, this time in the thrilling Series between Atlanta and Minnesota, with the hometown Twins facing elimination. In the bottom of the eleventh inning, having already saved at least a run with a spectacular catch in center field, Kirby Puckett led off with a line drive that easily cleared the Plexiglas wall in left-center to win the game. As the ball disappeared, Jack Buck, the broadcaster on CBS, simply said: "And we'll see you tomorrow night."

Joe Buck said after the 2011 game that he had not scripted any words in advance of Game Six's climax, aware of the dangers of canned material in a live broadcast. The touching symmetry was highlighted when his mother called him in the broadcast booth shortly after the game ended.

There are very few high-stakes games that have ended the way the two games in Minneapolis and St. Louis did, with so-called walk-off home runs, hits that literally win a game. Through 2012, only fourteen others have been hit in the long history of the World Series. Indeed, there had not been a single walk-off home run in the Series until Game One in 1949, when the Yankees' Tommy Henrich led off the ninth inning by putting one in the right-field seats off the Dodgers' Don Newcombe to break a scoreless tie.

Only two of these sixteen home runs have ended a

World Series—the Bill Mazeroski blast in the ninth inning that ended Game Seven against the Yankees in 1960 and Joe Carter's three-run blast against the Phillies in a 1993 Game Six win that produced the Blue Jays' second consecutive championship. That Carter home run, moreover, is only the second walk-off home run (the term did not come into use until the nineties) that not only won a World Series game but also erased a deficit, the other being the heroic hit by the injured Kirk Gibson in 1988.

Fortunately, none of the walk-off home runs in the World Series was cheap. Mazeroski's answer to Yankee Ralph Terry's second pitch was never in doubt as it sailed over the left-center field fence. Carlton Fisk's towering treatment of Pat Darcy's second pitch was clearly gone, the only question being whether it would drift foul as the Red Sox catcher famously waved his arms, urging it toward fair territory; and Freese's home run in 2011 was a vicious line drive to straightaway center field, on a full count against Ranger reliever Mark Lowe, which simply kept rising toward that welcoming patch of grass.

It is impossible for fans with a sense of history to think of one of these home runs without stirring memories of the others. Each shares an excruciating intensity, a heightened sensitivity, and an attention to detail that combine to produce the ineffable experience that unites baseball and religion. Modern television, with its multiple cameras and crowd close-ups, did not record the faces of those present for Mazeroski's shot in 1960; still, many who were not in the ballpark can attest to the deep intensity of the moment and to the movement of the experience from concentration to amazement and, finally, to awe. Today, as the experience builds, television reveals to millions clearly the faces of those involved—eyes burning, more than one pair watching the action through spread fingers. For fans and players, time slows and the moment builds within, a blend of nervous tension and sharpened focus, odds and tactics changing pitch-to-pitch, situation-to-situation, with the infinite possibilities of the game. Then, finally, ultimate release; ecstasy or agony, home run or strikeout. In those moments, bonds are forged, memories are made, and the game's revelatory capacity appears in powerful form as player and fan transcend the profane and meet the sacred. And in those moments lie experiences and lessons familiar to religious man.

In religious traditions, ritual and nostalgia merge, conjuring the long-ago event in sacred time. In secular affairs, memory is central. Sometimes it comes in a flash; often it is cultivated and preserved by families, friends, even societies. The past and present are more clearly linked, one enhancing and informing the experience of the other. The observation near the beginning of Ecclesiastes that nothing is new under the sun may not be quite true, but the dialogue between present and past often is inexhaustible, even as it causes us to touch a spot deep within ourselves.

In 2011, tens of millions of people shook their heads in amazement when Freese put a huge exclamation point on the Cardinals' comeback victory. But for those who truly see the game, Freese was not simply channeling Mazeroski, Fisk, Gibson, or Puckett; for thousands of baseball fans he was re-creating their magic. In a way, Freese *was Fisk*. The nostalgia of baseball, the timeless sport, evokes always the eternal return. The ghosts that Derek Jeter murmured about to Aaron Boone just before yet another miracle in 2003 are always close at hand—thank God.

For those who love gospel music—and what sentient human being doesn't—there is an especially wonderful tune that is still played after more than sixty years. "Life Is a Ball Game" was first introduced in the early fifties by a legend, Sister Wynona Carr. In addition to performing and recording, her duties included directing the choir at New Bethel Baptist Church in Detroit, where the Reverend C. L. Franklin, Aretha's father, preached.

In her foot-stomping classic, first base is temptation, second base is sin, and third is tribulation. But, of course, "Jesus is standing at the home plate, he's waiting for you there."

The pitcher is Satan, Solomon is the umpire, and the leadoff man is Daniel, who gets the first hit. The game's home run is hit by Job, wielding the "strong bat" of prayer. The chorus ends with a rousing "Life is a ball game, but you've got to play it fair."

These metaphors and symbols are powerful. They unite

baseball and God. By contrast, there will be no song based upon the material from my class at NYU. In our work, we have fixed on lessons at once more theoretical and ecumenical. We focus on two words, one an adjective, the other a noun, each written on the blackboard in the opening moments of the first day of class and each connecting the worlds of baseball and religion.

The adjective: *ineffable*. That which we know through experience rather than through study, that which ultimately is indescribable in words yet is palpable and real. The word signifies the truths known in the soul.

Alan Watts, who fifty years ago helped to popularize the religions of the Far East in the United States and whose works on Taoism, Buddhism, and Zen are still classics, put it this way: Trying to capture these truths through logic alone involves trying "to speak the unspeakable, scrute the inscrutable, and eff the ineffable."

Stories are better. For example, Derek Jeter flipping that ball sideways to Jorge Posada during the 2001 playoffs or Sandy Amoros sprinting toward that fly ball hit by Yogi Berra in 1955 or the catch you had with your father, or mother, or brother, or sister, or best friend.

The noun: *hierophany*. Mircea Eliade's term, derived from the Greek for a manifestation of the sacred or holy. A hierophany produces a moment of spiritual epiphany and connection to a transcendent plane. A heightened sensitivity opens us to this manifestation of the sacred in ordinary life. There is, in these hierophanic moments, a sharp divergence in feeling and awareness, space and time, from our profane experiences.

Eliade used hierophany as a companion to the word theophany—a manifestation of what most religious people label God. Hierophany is a broader term, encompassing what we might consider the spiritual, as opposed to a more specific and, in some traditions, more personal (and anthropomorphic) word *God*. It points to the experience of being transformed and elevated, going beyond self and the physical world—what William James pondered in much of his work as he tried, in his words, to "reduce religion to its lowest admissible terms, to that minimum, free from individualistic excrescences, which all religions contain at their nucleus."

And herein lies the point: The deeply profound experience captured by the words *ineffable* and *hierophany* is not the exclusive province of organized religion. For some, indeed, for a great many, it can be evoked at mass; but for others, the spark can be a Beethoven symphony; for others still, a Sandy Koufax breaking ball. As James Joyce wrote in *Ulysses*, "Any object, intensely regarded, may be a gate of access to the incorruptible eon of the gods." Any stone, as Eliade taught, can be a sacred stone.

Many students of religion and the game have attempted to connect Eliade's concept of the sacred stone with baseball's "rock." Such attempts have produced some memorable writing, for example this over-the-top description of baseball offered by theologian David Bentley Hart in his essay "A Perfect Game":

> I know there are those who will accuse me of exaggeration when I say this, but until baseball appeared, humans were a sad and benighted lot, lost in the labyrinth of matter, dimly and achingly aware of something incandescently beautiful and unattainable, something infinitely desirable shining up above in the empyrean of the ideas. . . .
>
> Part of the deeper excitement of the game is following how the strategy is progressively altered, from pitch to pitch, cumulatively and prospectively, in accordance both with the situation of the inning and the balance of the game. There is nothing else

like it, for sheer progressive intricacy, in all of sport. Comparing baseball to even the most complex versions of the oblong game [football] is like comparing chess to tiddlywinks.

And surely some account has to be given of the drama of baseball: the way it reaches down into the soul's abysses with its fluid alterations of prolonged suspense and shocking urgency, its mounting rallies, its thwarted ventures, its intolerable tensions, its suddenly exhilarating or devastating peripeties. . . . And because, until the final out is recorded, no loss is an absolute *fait accompli,* the torment of hope never relents. Victory may or may not come in a blaze of glorious elation, but every defeat, when it comes, is sublime. The oblong game is war, but baseball is Attic [Greek] tragedy.

All of this, it seems to me, points beyond the game's physical dimensions and toward its immense spiritual horizons.

No one has described the profound dimensions of baseball better, or with more eloquence and insight, than the late Bart Giamatti—Renaissance man, scholar, university president (at Yale), devoted family man (his son is the actor Paul Giamatti), and, finally commissioner of baseball, the one time we've had a commissioner who loved the game more than the business, who emphasized stewardship rather than ownership. After his premature death in 1989 at age fifty-one, friends put together a collection of his baseball writings and speeches and called it *A Great and Glorious Game.*

It is a great and glorious volume, beginning with a keen observation about baseball's almost casually cruel arithmetic: "It breaks your heart. It is designed to break your heart. The game begins in the spring, when everything else begins again, and it blossoms in the summer, filling the afternoons and evenings, and then as soon as the chill rains come, it stops and leaves you to face the fall alone." Giamatti wrote that it "keeps time fat and slow and lazy." As he noted correctly, "In 1839, the rule became fixed that one runs [the bases] counterclockwise. Time does not matter in baseball."

Giamatti was writing after his beloved Red Sox had just missed in another pennant race, but his wistful words mask an abiding hope for the next spring and the profound optimism it will bring: "I was counting on the game's deep patterns, three strikes, three outs, three times three innings, and its deepest impulse, to go out and back, to leave and to return home, to set the order of the day and to organize the daylight." A continual theme in Giamatti's prose concerns the importance of the concept of home in baseball, especially in a nation as peripatetically bustling as America. He summed up his inspiring worldview in an essay about the Sox–Yankees playoff game in 1978, which featured a wonderful analogy: Each batter, for him, is Odysseus.

> Baseball is about homecoming. It is a journey by theft and strength, guile and speed, out around first to the far island of second, where foes lurk in the reefs and the green sea suddenly grows deeper, then to turn sharply, skimming the shallows, making for a shore that will show a friendly face, a color, a familiar language and, at third, to proceed, no longer by paths indirect but straight, to home.
>
> Baseball is about going home, and how hard it is to get there and how driven is our need. It tells us how good home is. Its wisdom says you can go home again but that you cannot stay. The journey must always start once more, the bat an oar over the shoulder, until there is an end to all journeying.

Nostos; the going home; the game of nostalgia, so apt an image for our hunger that it hurts.

Giamatti's writings about baseball fit in a long line of writing about the elevating capacity of the game that can be traced back at least to Walt Whitman. In 1846, as the rules of baseball and the nation's love for it still were evolving, the great poet's observations were recorded at least twice:

"In our sundown perambulations of late through the outer parts of Brooklyn, we have observed several parties of youngsters playing 'base,' a certain game of ball. . . . The game of ball is glorious. . . . I see great things in baseball. It is our game, the American game. Baseball will take people out of doors, fill them with oxygen, give them a larger physical stoicism, tend to relieve us from being a nervous, dyspeptic set, repair those losses and be a blessing to us."

From a different perspective, I have tried to show how many of the elements we find in baseball—faith, doubt, conversion, accursedness, blessings—are elements associated with the religious experience; that inside the game the formative material of spirituality can be found. In short, viewed through a certain lens, baseball evokes the essence of religion. If we open ourselves to the rhythms and intricacies of the game, if we sharpen our noticing capacity, if we allow the timelessness and intensity of the game's most magnificent moments to shine through, the resulting heightened sensitivity might give us a sense of the ineffable, the transcendent.

Baseball is defined by wonder and amazement: Johnny Podres's proud ironworker father from upstate New York, ducking out of the Brooklyn Dodgers' clubhouse celebration after Game Seven in 1955, crying alone in the players' parking lot after his son's astonishing game against the

Yankees. This wonder and amazement, this touching of the beyond, is not the domain of the unknown that will someday be known but the domain of the unknowable, of faith.

But in baseball as in religion, deep faith cannot exist unless there is doubt, its handmaiden; confronting doubt is a central challenge in both religion and life, from the earliest Christian theologians to the 1991 Braves and Twins. This journey takes many roads, but conversion is certainly one of them, and the last steps can be truly miraculous as well as inexplicable. But there is a fine line between agony and ecstasy. Had Willie Mays dropped that fly ball in 1954, Giants fans may well have considered themselves accursed rather than blessed. It helps as well when our heroes are good people and not simply accomplished. Without sinners, our saints would be unremarkable. For each Christy Mathewson, there is often a Ty Cobb. We also want to try to keep them alive, to revisit their stories, both to learn from them and to try to relive their magic. It is no disrespectful sacrilege to observe that Jews gather for Passover Seders each year to re-create the miraculous story of their release from slavery in Egypt and that Pirates fans gather every October to experience Bill Mazeroski's home run again. And as in religion, some of the most meaningful experiences in baseball are not lived alone but are shared with communities—from a family to a team to a country—that unite us in concentric circles of relationship.

My NYU course and this book are attempts at exploring the basic building blocks of a spiritual or religious life, finding them, perhaps surprisingly to some, in an institution associated with secular life. The nine innings of this book are an assertion—an affirmation—that there is a meaningful dimension of the human experience (whether seen in what we recognize formally as religions or in a secular pursuit called baseball) that cannot be captured in words. Francis Bacon once observed, "The best part of beauty is that which a picture cannot express." This dimension, which coexists with the dimension of the known, the knowable, and the wonder of science, affirms some of the most important truths of our humanity, like the joy of love or the significance of our lives. This reflection won't persuade those who are not at some level already aware of it. As Louis Armstrong once said of jazz: "If you have to ask what it is, you'll never know."

In our times, it is fashionable to force a choice between the worlds of science and religion, of the mind and the soul. Either/or. This, in my view, is a false dichotomy—and perhaps this collection of baseball stories analyzed through a lens (and an intellectual tradition) usually reserved for the study of what are obviously religious experiences can cause some to see why. I embrace enthusiastically the joys of the intellectual life; but I reject the notion that, as a consequence, I must forfeit the wonders of a deeply transformative religious life.

Baseball calls us to live slow and notice. This alone may be enough—if it causes some to perceive the world differently and more intensely. The game answers the call issued by my late teacher, the Passionist (referring to the Catholic order) priest and cultural historian Thomas Berry, when he wrote that "when we see a flower, a butterfly, a tree, when we feel the evening breeze flow over us or wade in a stream of clear water, our natural response is immediate, intuitive, transforming, ecstatic. Everywhere we find ourselves invaded by the world of the sacred."

Father Berry's words struck a chord with me years ago. I grew up in New York's Rockaways, with a great beach and the beautiful Atlantic as backdrop to all we did. It was not a neighborhood for the economic upper class, but all of us were enriched beyond measure by the beautiful infinitude that stretched before us at the beach wall. As the physicist Richard Feynman, who also grew up in the Rockaways, put it: "If we stand on the shore and look at the sea, we see the water, the waves breaking, the foam, the sloshing motion of the water, the sound, the air, the winds and the clouds, the sun and the blue sky, and light; there is sand and there are rocks of various hardness and permanence, color and texture. There are animals and seaweed, hunger and disease, and the observer on the beach; there may be even happiness and thought."

Such meditations prepare us to probe the ineffable wonders of life—through science and religion, in concert not in conflict.

In encouraging my students to see the world in this way, I have sought to provoke, not to preach. For some of my students, an exploration of baseball and the experiences, impulses, and feelings it provokes has prompted a way of looking at the world that makes them more capable of embracing ineffable joys, even as they develop the life of the mind.

Beyond this, studying the game as we do reveals how structural elements we associate with religion often are present in the apparently mundane. In this way, baseball illustrates the nature of the religious experience. This may cause some to investigate further. And that would be good.

Unrestrained by time, baseball encourages, almost requires in its most meaningful moments, an appreciation of living slowly and in the moment; the kind of differentiated experience that separates the sacred in life from the profane. This experience is where religion begins. As Rabbi Heschel wrote, it "is not a feeling for the mystery of living, or a sense of awe, wonder, or fear, which is the root of religion; but rather the question *what to do* with the feeling for the mystery of living, what to do with awe, wonder, or fear." In a way, baseball's window into the nature of religious experience is more revelatory, frankly, than the window offered by much of organized religion.

There are difficulties, of course, associated with the word *religion*—and much evil has come from attempting to take the religious experience and "explain" it—that is, to codify it in dogma. Wars have erupted over that dogma. A lust for power and greed has allowed the sanctification of the material world in God's name: How high is one's steeple? How much gold is in one's chalice? All this for the greater glorification of something that is quite profane— something that can be labeled God but is anything but God in the sense that the greatest thinkers and lovers of religion use the word.

As beloved, sanctified even, as are Hall of Fame ballplayers, championship teams, and revered figures of the game, there has always existed a matter of perspective in baseball. Arguments sometimes are heated. Thankfully, however, nobody ever had to go to war over the Babe.

But this book in the end is simply a vehicle to tell some stories that reveal a love of baseball—and (in some of the stories) display the joy of a spiritual life. And maybe it shows that it is possible, even for a committed intellectual, to embrace both. It is, to repeat Tillich's words, "to convince some readers of the hidden power of faith within themselves and of the infinite significance of that to which faith is related."

Baseball can reveal something about the world and our ways of living in it that goes beyond what we see on the field. It can teach us to notice and embrace the ineffable beyond, to find the sacred amidst the profane. Just ask yourself: Do you, as you read these stories of baseball, see or recognize elements you associate with religion and the spiritual life? Do you see things here that resonate with you in some dimension of your being, which might add value to your life? Do you see a way of looking at the world that might be useful? If so, baseball perhaps is a guide to viewing religion and the spiritual life differently, to living differently, to being in the world in a different way and seeing more in it.

Okay. Baseball, for most of us anyway, is not *the* road to God—indeed, it is not even *a* road to God. But, if given sensitive attention, it can awaken us to a dimension of life often missing in our contemporary world of hard facts and hard science. We can learn, through baseball, to experience life more deeply. By embracing the ineffable joys of the "green fields of the mind," we can enlarge our capacity to embrace the ineffable more generally. Baseball can teach us that living simultaneously the life of faith and the life of the mind is possible, even fun.

And each winter, as we long for the possibilities of spring with its awakening, and as we ponder the depths of mystical moments past in baseball and in life, we proclaim our creed:

Wait'll Next Year!

ACKNOWLEDGMENTS

T his book has been a true collaboration. It linked the
president of New York University and the creator of its
popular course, Baseball as a Road to God, with a
writer and frequent guest in the course, and with another
writer who has assisted in the teaching of it after being its
first enrolled student a decade ago. Building on the course
and the insights and stories that form its core, we spent
scores of hours discussing concepts, topics, and details in-
depth together. We researched together. We discussed some
more together. We wrote together. We revised together. And
we rewrote together.

Along the way we have incurred huge debts. Above all,
we thank two close friends, each of whom has joined John
in teaching the course at various times over the years: Michael Murray and James Traub. They added immeasurably
to its content and meaning. And we thank the dozens of
NYU students who have given the course life.

We are also indebted to those who gave time and effort

to provide us with essential guidance, criticism, and assistance, including professors Jules Coleman and Arthur Miller, Paige Gilliam, Keith Sabalja, Deborah Grosvenor (our literary representative), and Patrick Mulligan (our editor at Gotham Books). And John's assistant, Dan Evans, who coordinated it all.

And we are grateful to those gentle critics who helped curb our tendencies toward verbosity and fuzziness, above all Alan and Arlene Schwartz, Susan Spencer, and Dr. Joan Witkin.

For detailed baseball information, our principal source was the multi-editioned *Baseball Encyclopedia*, going elsewhere only when necessary. All this help, however, does not absolve us of total responsibility for any errors contained in these pages.

John Sexton, Thomas Oliphant,
and Peter J. Schwartz

Want to continue traveling along baseball's road? Check out some of these works that have been assigned over the years in my NYU seminar.

BOOKS

The Art of Fielding, Chad Harbach

Brooklyn's Dodgers, Carl E. Prince

Calico Joe, John Grisham

The Celebrant, Eric Rolfe Greenberg

The Chosen, Chaim Potok

Cosmos and History, Mircea Eliade

The Era, 1947–1957, Roger Kahn

Fair Ball: A Fan's Case for Baseball, Bob Costas

The Further Adventures of Slugger McBatt, W. P. Kinsella

Go the Distance, W. P. Kinsella

God in Search of Man, Abraham Joshua Heschel

A Great and Glorious Game, A. Bartlett Giamatti

Homo Ludens, Johan Huizinga

Honest to God, John A. T. Robinson

If Wishes Were Horses, W. P. Kinsella

The Iowa Baseball Confederacy, W. P. Kinsella

The Joy of Sports, Michael Novak

Magic Time, W. P. Kinsella

The Natural, Bernard Malamud

The Old Man and the Sea, Ernest Hemingway

Past Time: Baseball as History, Jules Tygiel

Praying for Gil Hodges, Thomas Oliphant

The Sacred and the Profane, Mircea Eliade

Shoeless Joe, W. P. Kinsella

Snow in August, Pete Hamill

Summer of '49, David Halberstam

Take Me Out, Richard Greenberg

Ultimate Concern, Paul Tillich

The Universal Baseball Association, Inc., J. Henry Waugh, Prop., Robert Coover

The Varieties of Religious Experience, William James

Wait Till Next Year, Doris Kearns Goodwin

Why Time Begins on Opening Day, Thomas Boswell

ARTICLES AND EXCERPTS

"Baseball: A Spiritual Reminiscence," Tex Sample

"Baseball and the Meaning of Life: Are We Destined to Grasp Neither?" Donald Hall

"Baseball as Civil Religion: The Genesis of an American Creation Story," Christopher Evans

"Believing in Baseball: The Religious Power of Our National Pastime," Thomas Dailey

Brain Droppings ("Baseball and Football"), George Carlin

"Civil Religion in America," Robert Bellah

"The Coming of Elijah: Baseball as Metaphor," William R. Herzog II

Flight of the Wild Gander ("Secularization of the Sacred"), Joseph Campbell

"God's Country and Mine," Jacques Barzun

Japanese Baseball ("The Indestructible Hadrian Wilks"), W. P. Kinsella

"The Kingdom of Baseball in America: The Chronicle of an American Theology," Christopher Evans

"Louisville Slugger Sure Sign of a Higher Power," George Will

"McDuff on the Mound," Robert Coover

The Meaning of Sports ("Baseball: The Remembrance of Things Past"), Michael Mandelbaum

"The Odds of That," *The New York Times Magazine*, August 11, 2002

"On Jackie Robinson," Red Barber

Selected Stories ("The Pitcher"), Andre Dubus

"The Silent Season of a Hero," Gay Talese

"Summer Dreams," Leonard Kriegel

"Tao in the Yankee Stadium Bleachers," John Updike

Underworld (prologue), Don DeLillo

"With Red Sox, Glass Is Always Half-Empty," *The New York Times*, September 3, 2004

FILM

Brooklyn Dodgers: The Ghosts of Flatbush (HBO)

Tippy, the maven who sometimes is wrong but never in doubt, offers the following trivia tidbits. As he does, he says: "You can take these to the bank." I suggest a fact-check, however, before you bet your home on their accuracy. Still, these pieces of baseball lore do reveal some of the game's wonder.

Certain "unbreakable" records, perennials on most fans' lists, are not included because Tippy takes them as part of every true fan's landscape. For example, Cy Young's 511 career wins, 316 career losses, and 749 career complete games; Jack Chesbro's 41 wins in a season (most since 1900); Hack Wilson's 191 RBIs in a season; or Joe DiMaggio's 56-game hitting streak.

© NYU Photo Bureau: Hollenshead

Human Baseball Encyclopedia: Anthony (Tippy)
Mannino, outside the friendly confines of his town car

TWENTY ABSOLUTELY
UNBREAKABLE RECORDS

———————— ◆ ————————

1. The Chicago Cubs and Cincinnati Reds played an entire nine-inning game (June 29, 1916) using only *one* baseball.
2. The Cleveland Indians played an entire game against the New York Yankees (July 5, 1945) without an infield assist.
3. Brooklyn (1920) holds the record for most innings played by a team over a three-game stretch: fifty-eight.
4. The New York Yankees played 308 consecutive games (August 3, 1931, to August 2, 1933) without being shut out.
5. The world-champion Pittsburgh Pirates (1960) had a collective ERA of 7.11 in the World Series, the worst ever by a Series participant, let alone a winning team.
6. Pete Rose (1963–86, Cincinnati Reds, Philadelphia Phillies, and Montreal Expos) played more than five hundred major league games at each of five different positions (first, second, and third base; right and left field).
7. Walter Johnson (Washington Senators) recorded nine consecutive seasons (1910–18) of pitching three hundred or more innings.
8. Walter Johnson also won thirty-eight 1–0 games in his career, a record. He lost twenty-six 1–0 games, also a record.
9. Christy Mathewson (1905 New York Giants) won three complete-game shutouts in the same World Series.
10. Babe Ruth (1916 Boston Red Sox) pitched fourteen innings in a World Series game, winning it 2–1.
11. Red Barrett (1944 Boston Braves) threw a complete game with only fifty-eight pitches; the game took seventy-five minutes from the first pitch to the last. The Giants and the Robins (later the Dodgers) took only fifty-seven minutes, first pitch to last out, to complete a nine-inning game, which the Giants won 1–0 (August 30, 1918).
12. Grover Cleveland Alexander (1916 Philadelphia Phillies) had sixteen shutouts in one season. Bob Gibson (1968 St. Louis Cardinals) had thirteen.
13. Greg Minton (1978–82 San Francisco Giants) pitched 269⅓ innings without giving up a home run.
14. Steve Carlton (1972 Philadelphia Phillies) won twenty-seven games for a last-place team, accounting for 46 percent of the team's victories for the season.
15. Leon Cadore (Brooklyn Robins) and Joe Oeschger (Boston Braves) pitched twenty-six innings each in the same game (May 1, 1920).

Honorable mention: Bob Smith (1927 Boston Braves) pitched twenty-two innings in a loss to the Cubs, still the longest complete game decision in National League history.

16. Walter Johnson (1925 Washington Senators) won twenty games and batted over .400 (.433) in the same season.

17. Sam Crawford (1899–1917, Cincinnati Reds and Detroit Tigers) recorded fifty-one inside-the-park home runs in his career.

18. Joe Sewell (1929 Cleveland Indians) played in 115 consecutive games, covering 437 at-bats, without striking out. In his fourteen-year career, covering more than seven thousand at-bats, Sewell struck out only 114 times.

19. Joel Youngblood (1982 New York Mets and Montreal Expos) is the only player to get a hit for two different teams on the same day. The games were in two different cities (Chicago and Philadelphia).

20. Branch Rickey (1907 New York Highlanders), playing as a catcher, yielded thirteen stolen bases in a game.

TWENTY BREAKABLE, BUT REALLY INTERESTING RECORDS

◆

1. The Boston Red Sox scored seventeen runs in a single inning (1953). The National League record is fifteen by the Brooklyn Dodgers (1952). In that May 20, 1952, game against Cincinnati, nineteen consecutive Dodgers reached base in an inning (it was the first inning).

2. The Pittsburgh Pirates beat the Chicago Cubs 22–0 (September 16, 1975), the most runs ever scored in a shutout win. The Cubs also scored 22 runs (in 1979) but lost 23–22 in ten innings to the Philadelphia Phillies, the forty-five runs being the highest total for any game.

3. The San Diego Padres used four different managers in a nine-inning game (August 12, 1984).

4. Phil Niekro (1979 Atlanta Braves) led his league in *both* wins and losses in the same season (twenty-one wins and twenty losses).

5. Johnny Vander Meer (1938 Cincinnati Reds) is the only pitcher to ever throw no-hitters in consecutive games. (Most pundits would say this belongs among the unbreakable records; Tippy views the achievement as more modest and cites Toronto's Dave Stieb, who came achingly close—only one out shy of tossing a no-hitter in back-to-back starts—fifty years later. Stieb joins only six other pitchers in the modern era who have pitched one-hitters in consecutive starts.)

6. Harvey Haddix (1959 Pittsburgh Pirates) pitched twelve perfect innings in a single game. The Milwaukee Braves finally got to him in the thirteenth, winning 1–0 with a complete game from their pitcher, Lew Burdette.

7. Mark Buehrle (2009 Chicago White Sox) retired forty-five consecutive batters over three games.

8. Bill Fischer (1962 Kansas City Athletics) recorded the most consecutive innings without walking a batter: 84⅓.

9. Pitcher Jim Tobin (1942 Boston Braves) hit three home runs in a game.

10. Pitcher Tony Cloninger (1966 Atlanta Braves) hit two grand slams in a game.

11. Rick Wise (1971 Philadelphia Phillies) pitched a no-hitter and also hit two home runs in the *same* game.

12. Ken Brett (1973 Philadelphia Phillies) hit home runs in four consecutive starts (his only four home runs of the season). He is the only pitcher ever to do it.

13. Cesar Tovar (1965–76 Minnesota Twins, Philadelphia Phillies, Texas Rangers, Oakland Athletics, and New York Yankees) spoiled five no-hitters by getting the only hit of the game.

14. Ted Williams (1957 Boston Red Sox) reached base sixteen consecutive times (six hits, nine walks, one hit by pitch). Pinky Higgins (1938 Red Sox) and Walt Dropo (1952 Detroit Tigers) had twelve consecutive at-bats with hits.

15. Paul Waner (1927 Pittsburgh Pirates) got an extra-base hit in fourteen consecutive games. Don Mattingly (1986 New York Yankees) holds the American League record at ten.

16. Vern Stephens (1953 Boston Red Sox) had three hits in a single inning.

17. Only two Hall of Fame players (Hoyt Wilhelm of the New York Giants and Earl Averill of the Cleveland Indians) hit homers in their first career at-bat. Over the years, 116 players have done it, twenty-eight on the first pitch. Four have done it with the bases loaded, one (Bill Duggleby) in 1898, and three in the first ten years of this century (Jeremy Hermida in 2005, Kevin Kouzmanoff in 2006, and Daniel Nava in 2010).

18. Roy Cullenbine (1947 Detroit Tigers) earned a base on balls in twenty-two consecutive games.

19. Johnny Gochnaur (1903 Cleveland Indians) recorded ninety-eight fielding errors in a season.

20. Babe Ruth (1926 New York Yankees) is the only player caught stealing to make the last out in a World Series. He was attempting to steal second base.

Index

Index

Index

and the New York Yankees, xiii,
47–49, 77, 79–81
and the Philadelphia Phillies, 87
Sexton on, xii–xiii
Tillich on, 93–94
Cooperstown, New York,
145, 178
Coover, Robert, 65–67
Coppola, Francis Ford, 101
Cosell, Howard, 190
Counsell, Craig, 122
Coveleski, Harry, 194
Coveleski, Stan, 194
Cox, Bobby, 114–15, 126
Cozart, Zack, 173
Crawford, Carl, 137
Crawford, Regular Rob, 85
Cronin, Joe, 136
Crosby, Bing, 27
Cuba, 156–57
cultural assimilation, 179–81
curses. See blessings and curses
cyclical time, 28

Daily Mirror, 77
Damon, Johnny, 149–50
Darcy, Pat, 208
Dark, Alvin, 106
data, 64–67. *See also* sabermetrics;
statistics
Davis, Chili, 114
Davis, Clive, 115
Davis, George "Iron," 117–18
Davis, Mike, 40–41
deadball era, 151
deception, 58–59
"Deep in the Heart of Texas," 169
Deism, 123
DeLillo, Don, 101–2
Denkinger, Don, 63
Dent, Bucky, 88
Denver, John, 170
desegregation of baseball, 135–36,
158, 194
Detroit Free Press, 180
Detroit Tigers
1934 World Series, 180–81
1968 World Series, 49–50
1988 World Series, 39
and blown calls, 62
and Cobb, 152
and Forbes Field, 24–25
and MVP Awards, 43
Deus Absconditus, 125

Dewey, John, 181–82
dhamma, 148
Dickey, R. A., 62
Didier, Mel, 41
dilemma, 96
DiMaggio, Joe
and hitting records, 65, 190
and nostalgic elements of
baseball, 197
and Opening Day, 29
and Yankees' tradition, 39, 47, 129
Dobrusin, Robert, 138
Doby, Larry, 106, 107
Dodger Stadium, 170–71
Doerr, Bobby, 197
dogma, 71–73, 219
Dolorosa, Maria, 99
Doubleday, Abner, 178
doubt, 53–76
and ambiguity, 59–63
and chance and statistics, 64–67
and faith, 54–58, 60–61, 67, 69,
71–74, 76, 216
and trivia, 67–76
Doubt: A Parable (Shanley), 58–59
Douglas, Bobby "Dougie," xi, 1–2, 7,
11–12, 14, 109–10, 143
drama of baseball, 213
Dreyfus, Hubert, 33, 177
Dreyfuss, Barney, 25
drug use in baseball, 162–63
Drysdale, Don, 78
duality, 66, 149
Durocher, Leo, 106, 108
Dykstra, Lenny, 149
Dynamics of Faith (Tillich), 94

Ebbets Field, 1n, 78, 84, 85, 87
Ecclesiastes, 209
Eckersley, Dennis, 31–32, 40–42, 44
ecumenism, 48
Einstein, Albert, 34–35, 66
Eisenhower, Dwight D., 90
Eliade, Mircea
and *axis mundi,* 21, 202
and hierophany, 8–9, 11–12, 16,
27–28, 211–12
and ineffable events, 89
and the *Myth of the Eternal
Return,* 30–31, 103–5, 204
and nostalgia, 200–201
and sacred places, 27–28
and spiritual epiphanies, 94
Emerson, Ralph Waldo, 51, 101

Index

Index

Good Samaritan parable, 61
Goodwin, Doris Kearns, 82–85, 96–97
gospel music, 210
Gospel of John, 123
Gospel of Matthew, 57, 195
Gould, Stephen Jay, 4–5, 65
Grace, Mark, 122
Graham, Archibald "Moonlight," 145, 187
grand slams, 67, 70, 76
Grant, M. Donald, 37
Grant, Ulysses S., 157
A Great and Glorious Game (Giamatti), 213–15
The Great Gatsby (Fitzgerald), 176
The Great God of Baseball (Hye), 156–57
Great Hall (Yankee Stadium), 20
"Green Light Letter" (Roosevelt), 182
Green Monster, 197
Greenberg, Eric Rolfe, 18–19, 154–55
Greenberg, Hank, 180–182
Grimes, Burleigh, 194
Grissom, Marv, 108
Guest, Edgar A., 181
Guidry, Ron, 197
Gullett, Don, 79

haftarah, 147
Hagar (biblical), 112
Hagy, "Wild" Bill, 169–70
Hall of Fame for Great Americans, 157
Hart, David Bentley, 212–13
Havana Heat (Brock), 156–57
Hebrew Scriptures, 123–24, 146–47
Hebrew University of Jerusalem, 99–100
Henrich, Tommy, 207
heroes. *See* saints and sinners
Hershberger, Willard, 198–99
Heschel, Abraham Joshua, 3, 7, 44, 57, 92, 146, 218
hierophany
  and conversion experiences, 89–90
  described, 8–9
  and doubt, 61
  Eliade's use of, 8–9, 11–12, 16, 27–28, 211–12
  and miracles, 99, 125
  and sacred places, 27–28
  and saints, 146

Hinduism, 56–57, 147–48
Hoak, Don, 15
Hobbs, Roy (fictional), 147, 159, 160, 163
Hodges, Gil
  1952 World Series, 131–32
  1955 World Series, 2, 110
  1956 World Series, 111–12
  1969 World Series, 74–75
  and conversion experiences, 85, 87
  and Hall of Fame voting, 148
  as Met manager, 47
  slumps, xii, 131–32
Hodges, Russ, 101–2
Hornsby, Rogers, 28–29
Houston Astros, 54, 169
Howard, Elston, 2, 190
Hoyt, Waite, 134
Hrbek, Kent, 116
Hubbell, Carl, 193
hubris, 12
Hunter, Catfish, 79
Hye, Allen E., 156–57

"I'll Be with You in Apple Blossom Time," 168
immigrant communities, 25–26, 189
Impossible Dream, 54, 89
Index of Forbidden Books, 73
ineffable events
  1955 World Series, 3
  and the 2004 Red Sox, 13–14
  and conversion experiences, 89–90, 92
  and definition of God, 10–11
  described, 211
  and doubt, 76
  and faith, 51
  Heschel on, 7, 44
  and hierophany, 8–9
  and miracles, 123, 125
  and nostalgic elements of baseball, 208
  and religious meaning, 212
  and sacred time, 34–35
  and science/religion dichotomy, 4–5, 218
  and spiritual power of baseball, 16, 219–20
  and transcendence, 215
inside-the-park grand slams, 67, 70
instant replay, 62
interleague play, 79, 197

Index

Index

Index